Stephanie Calman is a writer and broadcaster whose 'Happy Families' column appears regularly in the *Daily Telegraph*. She is also the creator of the hugely popular website www.badmothersclub.com and she appears regularly on TV and radio. She is still married to author Peter Grimsdale, with whom she has two children.

HOW NOT TO MURDER YOUR HUSBAND

Stephanie Calman demonstrates, with devastating precision, how very, very, annoying husbands are, and examines the alternatives such as adultery — 'All I'd want to do in a hotel room is order room service' — before concluding how incredible it is that anyone manages to stay married at all. Drawing on moments from her own marriage to the man 'everyone else thinks is perfect', who — among his other crimes — 'breathes like Darth Vader when asleep, but not in a sexy, black cloak, galaxy-ruling sort of way, and always sees the other side in an argument' i.e., the side that isn't hers . . .

STEPHANIE CALMAN

NOT
HOW ʰ TO
MURDER YOUR
HUSBAND

Complete and Unabridged

ULVERSCROFT
Leicester

First published in Great Britain in 2010 by
Pan Books
an imprint of Pan Macmillan
London

First Large Print Edition
published 2011
by arrangement with
Pan Macmillan
London

British Library CIP Data

Calman, Stephanie.
    How not to murder your husband.
    1. Husbands- -Humor.
    2. Man-woman relationships- -Humor.
    3. Large type books.
    I. Title
    306.8'722'0207–dc22

    ISBN 978–1–44480–555–0

Published by
F. A. Thorpe (Publishing)
Anstey, Leicestershire

Set by Words & Graphics Ltd.
Anstey, Leicestershire
Printed and bound in Great Britain by
T. J. International Ltd., Padstow, Cornwall

This book is printed on acid-free paper

To Peter
As I said on July 16, 1994:
'All that I am, I give to you.'

Sorry about that.

How many married couples does it take to change a light bulb?
None.
Just the husband to say:
'I'll do it tomorrow.'
And the wife to say:
'My mother was right about you.'

Do you ever wake up thinking:

The sun is shining; it's Sunday morning; I don't have to pack anyone's swimming kit or build a cutaway of a volcano out of plaster of Paris. I'm going to greet the person lying next to me with sweetness and appreciation, anticipate his needs and offer him something really nice like scrambled eggs in bed or sex?

And within moments of thinking that, have you sat up and said:

'You woke me up with your bloody snoring again'?

If you answered *Yes*, then this book is for you.

CONTENTS

Acknowledgements

Thank you to George Morley and Mark Lucas, who helped make this book what it is, and to Peter who proved that he is perfect after all by letting us publish it. And an extra thank you to Mark for representing us both, though in the event of divorce I get custody of him.

My thanks also go to those who kindly revealed the inner workings of their own marriages on condition of anonymity, for entirely understandable reasons. And my mother, Pat McNeill, for describing both her marriage and her divorce, neither of which made the final cut, and for not minding about it.

And those who made the life of this working mother possible: Katarina, Hattie, Meriel, Hugo, Rebecca, Jane, Patrick, Ritchye and the Bridges — not of Madison County: of Crystal Palace — and Perfect Peter of course.

Lawrence and Lydia: so brilliant and funny. Soon you will be writing your own books, God help me.

Sophie Doyle, for managing to steer a path

through the detritus of two writers' lives.

An even bigger thank you to Lucy, and to Jon for being such a sport.

Relate, who answered the phone when we needed them to.

John Miller.

Graham Cave.

The TCCR and Maureen Boerma.

Christopher Clulow, who read and checked, and gave generously of his time.

Susie Orbach.

Jon Stock, in whose *Weekend Telegraph* pages a few fragments of this book first appeared.

Also Rachel Johnson at the *Lady*, and the features team at the *Daily Mail*, where some of the material about the accident was first published.

Roger Symes, Ian Moody and the other exes — you know who you are.

1

That Sinking Feeling

Peter and I are sitting on a low, squashy sofa in the front room of a nice, old terraced house with interestingly carved objects and intriguing little boxes on a coffee table to one side. Through the glass double doors we can see a small but beautifully landscaped garden full of lush, tropical plants: a tiny paradise amid the unrelenting autumn rain. The garden looks unattainable and slightly unreal, as though, if I went towards it, it might disappear. I feel as though I am sinking, and not just because of the sofa.

'He constantly undermines me in front of the children,' I say.

'No I don't.'

'You never back me up.'

'That's not true.'

'When he wants to get out of doing something, like talking to the bank or complaining to the school, he says, 'I'm putting you in charge of that', as if he's empowering me as a woman, when it just means he doesn't want to do it.'

'What do you mean? You never do that stuff! You profess to be the tough one, but you leave all the difficult conversations to me.'

'What a lie! You always say you'll 'give it some thought' — and nothing happens. Then it's too late!'

'I rang BT about the Broadband. Spent hours on the phone to India.'

'One hour. Once.'

'Twice, actually. And I drove back to photograph that parking sign so we could contest the ticket. And I got that £250 compensation from the bank.'

This is typical. You see what he's doing, sounding all marvellous and *reasonable*? That's all part of it. I examine the face of the man in the chair opposite for signs that he's being taken in. Everyone thinks Peter is so damn reasonable — that's partly why I'm here. I need someone to know, to acknowledge, how demoralizing it can be to live with a man who believes himself to be 100 per cent *good*. You used to hear of vicars' wives going bonkers and turning to drink; I know how they felt.

'I was the one who sat for ages in front of iPhoto downloading hundreds of pictures to find the parking sign because he hadn't deleted any of them — and refuses to learn how to do it. The bank, well, yeah, he did write all those letters and get that money. But so what? It's always presented as some huge favour all the time, as if it's really my job but he's taking it on because I've failed. 'What do you want?' I say. 'A medal?''

'Huh, and no,' he says, 'I don't back you up all the time when you bark at the children about their table manners, because it's so often completely unnecessary. Like when they're just trying to tell us about their day, and in you come like a sergeant major.'

We both know that we hardly argue at all when we're not with the children, but we don't say this because we love them so much. It would sound as though we don't want them, whereas one thing we never ever disagree about is how fantastic they are. And yet — so many of our arguments seem to be sparked by, or about, them.

'Oh, listen to yourself,' I say. 'When they're arguing at the table, or being really rude to me, you just let them. So of course I have to snap at them. I've got no choice. If you just showed them it was unacceptable I could back off. You know that perfectly well. But you're such a passive-aggressive.'

'And you're just aggressive.'

I glare at him. He may think this is in some way amusing. It is not.

'At least I admit I get angry. You just

present a totally false front. He *does*!'

I appeal to the man opposite. He assents slightly by way of a faint smile.

'Do you think that's fair, Peter?'

'Not really.'

Of course he doesn't: that's why we're here. Twenty years on the clock, fifteen since the wedding, and we're back in relationship counselling. Again.

2

Marriage Guidance by the SAS

The first time we went for help, we weren't even married yet, just living together. Graham was a social worker by training who'd seen just about every kind of awfulness families can inflict on each other, and did a lot of work in prisons. His approach was bracingly direct. Presented with a complaint from one of us about the other, for example Peter saying:

'Stephanie moaned at me about how bad her day was before I'd even taken off my coat', he'd lean forward, stare fiercely at the offending party, in this instance me, and bark:

'Well, did you?'

'Um, yes.'

'Well, don't. Leave it half an hour before you say any of that stuff.'

It was an amazingly effective technique, so much so that after we'd been married a few years we went back.

We'd reached a very low ebb and couldn't even speak to each other, it seemed, without sniping.

'If you go on like this,' he said, 'you won't have a marriage.'

It was marriage guidance by the SAS.

⋆ ⋆ ⋆

A couple of years back, we mentioned to a friend that we'd had counselling.

'Oh, I'm sorry,' he said. 'I had no idea.'

We had to convince him that not only were we not on the verge of divorce, we were also actually — thanks partly to the counselling — getting on quite well. But you can see his point; if you see a friend at the dentist, you do tend to assume they've got something wrong with their teeth. I suppose our policy is to go when we have toothache, rather than wait for the abscess to form. Anyway, isn't toothache itself awful enough?

One day I heard an interview on the radio with the woman who was then in charge of Relate. She regretted the fact that many couples only seek help as a last resort.

'I just wish,' she said, 'that people would come to us *before* it's terminal.'

After Graham we bumbled on not too badly for the next eight years or so, until we got derailed again. Lawrence and Lydia were still small, and far more high maintenance than they are now, if considerably less sarcastic, and we felt the burden of work, school and childcare far more heavily. Somewhere along the way we forgot how to be nice, and had got into the habit of routinely snapping at each other over nothing, like repeatedly crashing gears.

But Graham had retired. And Peter was prejudiced against normal counsellors on the grounds that they were too earnest. He always referred to them — only half-jokingly — as the 'noddy, smiley brigade', i.e. the sort of people who, if you tell them you've been hit by a car, will ask in an unnaturally neutral voice, '*And how do you feel about that?*'

Of course, having had both, I knew that he was thinking of psychotherapists. Of that lot it's definitely true. They don't give their opinion lest they 'lead the witness' and tell you what to think, and frustrating as it is, it works. Counsellors can give advice. And once Peter had decided that I had 'an anger problem' we had to go.

This time we had Sam, who was, rather to our surprise, charming, funny and glamorous.

'Are you allowed to find your counsellor beautiful?' said Peter after our first visit.

'Absolutely,' I said, 'so long as you don't sleep with her.'

I reminded him of the Monty Python sketch in which Michael Palin, as the drab

7

husband, burbles on monotonously as Eric Idle, the smooth-talking marriage guidance counsellor, seduces his wife.

'Except,' I said, 'it wouldn't be funny.'

Sam saw us in a small room right at the top of the old London Marriage Guidance building. To get there we had to climb a huge number of stairs, and always arrived panting heavily. So the sessions always started with a joke. It was always the same joke, but that's marriage for you.

She could see our problems weren't terminal; the relationship had simply run into the skirting board like a clockwork toy and just needed turning round. Talking things through with her, we were reminded of why we still preferred each other's company to that of anyone else. Also, when you're nurturing others twenty-four hours a day, it feels really nice to have someone care about *you*.

When Sam died, far too young, of cancer, we agreed that no matter how badly we might argue or fall out in the future, we'd never want to talk to anyone else. So there was no alternative: we'd just *have* to get on.

Which we did, more or less, if you don't count the sarcasm (him), the impatience (me), smugness and complacency (him), micro-management (me), refusal to address non-domestic conflicts, e.g. school (him) and assorted disagreements in general, until we found ourselves back at Square One again, in a counsellor's room.

This time the pressure was really on, as Peter was going away — only for a week, but he kept flying in and out of my office saying, 'We have to get this sorted in the next twenty-four hours!' like a character in *Spooks*.

'You do know it won't be solved in one session, don't you?' I told him. 'It's not like getting a new clutch.'

He bent down and looked at me witheringly.

'I don't want to go away leaving things like this. OK?'

'*Okay*-uh!' I replied, like Lydia in full sulk.

London Marriage Guidance had vanished by then so I looked up Relate, which began life in 1938 as the Marriage Guidance Council, to tackle 'the strain modern life was having on couple relationships and marriage', and was immediately deluged with potential clients. But surely everything was lovely in the good old days, when everyone knew their neighbours and the extended family was always there for you with a shoulder and a hot kettle to lean on.

Yeah, *right*.

Today their website glows with the confidence of the market leader:

'Relate the relationship people — we're

here to help you find the answers.'

It's so reassuringly *definite*, like an ad for a religion, or the police.

While I was at it, I also put in a call to the Tavistock Centre in north London. Where Relate is good quality but more 'high street', the Tavi is where you go if you want to delve more deeply. For example, if your husband wants to have sex with you dressed up as Mussolini, or you come home to find him sitting in the dark in a rocking chair, speaking in a high voice and dressed as his dead mother, you'd take him there.

While waiting for someone on the Relate list to get back to me, and to take the opportunity to find out roughly how typical — or abnormal — we were, I asked the Tavi to tell me the most common reasons relationships break down, and got this reply:

1. Inability to cope with change, i.e. rigid, inflexible relationship dynamic in the face of life events such as death, redundancy or serious illness.
2. Fear of dependency/commitment.
3. Inability to contain/manage conflict.
4. Difficulty managing children and/or their departure.
5. Unequal personal development, i.e. growing apart.

6. Inability to recover from disappointed expectations/ideals.

Well, I don't know about you, but my first reaction was: shit, I've got the lot. Then I calmed down a bit and remembered that I tend to be like the hypochondriac in *Three Men in a Boat* who thinks he's got every disease in the medical dictionary. And I got it down to two out of six: numbers three and four. And it was comforting to see number two there, proving that I'm not the only person who's ever suffered from *that*. I also noticed that 'meeting someone younger and more attractive' — which quite a few people seem to fear, especially women — was not on the list. And numbers one and six, which I think people under-estimate as a challenge, were. What they didn't include, however, was:

7. One or other spouse being passive-aggressive, his own ghastly spin doctor and massively bloody SMUG.

Let me tell you what I have to put up with.
A couple of years back, I had a drink with a woman who asked me,
'Are you as horrible to Peter in person as you are behind his back?'
And I said,

'Ha ha! Worse!'
And she said,
'God, *really?*'

Friends of ours, particularly males, and come to think of it females, love to take me aside at dinners, or outside the school gate, or wherever, and tell me how lucky I am. It's a generally accepted view amongst all who know us, apparently, that Peter is Perfect. One of them, when I was encouraging her to stick up for herself in her marriage, even once retorted snappishly:

'We can't all be married to Peter, you know!'

So I've decided to explode the myth of Super-spouse once and for all. Living intimately with another individual over a prolonged period leads to stress — and is, if you have children, frequently impossible. But are we two uniquely unable to bite our tongues? Do we really argue more than other couples? To say out loud the unsayable, has it all been a dreadful mistake?

3

The Bell Curve

One Sunday morning we're in one of our favourite local cafés, having a child-free breakfast before collecting Lawrence and Lydia from their respective sleepovers. And almost immediately we sit down, I become aware of a man at a nearby table dismembering his baguette, laying out the bacon, tomatoes and so on round the plate. And I think, if I were married to him, would I think that was sweet and endearing, or revolting?

'Do you think,' I ask Peter, 'that if someone does something like that on a first date it totally puts you off, but if they do it in the honeymoon period, when you adore them unreservedly, it's rather cute, then later on — '

'It's revolting again. You had no table manners when we met,' he adds, unnecessarily.

'What?! Because I once ate a lettuce leaf straight from the salad bowl?'

This was in the early days, when I was still thinking I might chuck him, on the very

13

reasonable grounds that he was extremely uptight.

'Exactly. You had no idea how to behave.'

Lovely. What began as a peaceful, Sunday morning coffee has turned into a dissection of my faults. I feel a strong urge to shove his *pain au raisin* in his face, except he hasn't yet eaten the squidgy middle bit which I fancy for myself.

'You're joking, right?'

'Either you've raised your standards or I've lowered mine.'

'Ah yes. This was around the same time as I first took you to my dad's cottage for the weekend and you had a go at me for eating a Mars Bar.'

We'd eaten at the usual sort of time, it was now around two hours later, and I felt like something sweet. So I nipped to the kitchen for some chocolate. And do you know what he said?

'We've only just had dinner!'

He said it with a horrified look, as if he'd caught me rummaging through the bin. I was quite slim at the time, certainly slimmer than I am now, but the way he looked at me — it was as though I'd stepped into the pages of Dickens:

'It's never been my policy to overfeed the female orphan, Mrs Sadist. It makes the blood rush to the head.'

'Quite right indeed, Mr Frightful. They were given mouldy bread only last Michaelmas and now here's one wanting more . . . '

That night I went to bed and lay there remembering an early boyfriend from my teens, who asked me to lose weight 'for him'. I was a bit over at the time, but only a bit: nothing you couldn't comfortably reach round. And anyway, that's obviously Not The Point. And though I had made a pact with myself that I would never again put up with any crap like that from a man, it seemed a pity to trash this promising new relationship over it. I strongly considered it over the bloody lettuce leaf, mind you.

Peter's one of those people who just doesn't binge, nibble, graze or — most frustratingly — put on weight, which makes it difficult for him to understand what it's like for those of us ordinary mortals who do. He doesn't even pig out at Christmas, due to his infuriating addiction to moderation.

I am very greedy, not just with food — with everything, and once I get started on a food I like, it's particularly hard to stop. Years ago I had a boyfriend whose mother made these wonderful Sunday lunches but only ever offered seconds to the men. Boyfriend and father would say 'no thank you' politely and I'd be left, after my modest female portion, listening to the individual molecules of ham salad or shepherd's pie pinging around in my rumbling tummy. We went there for Christmas once, and after I'd finished my supermodel-sized meal and everything had been cleared away, his parents went to bed. He and I stayed up to watch TV and I popped into the larder; there was literally half the turkey left. So I took a bit, then another bit, then I got a bigger knife and hacked away, sort of forgetting where I was. Then I heard the door open. His mother had come down for a drink of water and, presumably startled by the gnawing sounds, found me there, teeth bared, illuminated in the white light like the cave-dwelling cannibals in *The Descent*. He's married to someone else now.

That said, I think Peter's right. Not that he's 'lowered his standards', as he so charmingly puts it, but that we have sort of met in the middle. He's lightened up quite a lot. Well, he must have, or I wouldn't still be here.

Mind you, he still gets at me. That he often just eats an apple for breakfast is very annoying. He almost *always* drinks sensibly and when I have a second drink — well, all right, a third or fourth — says,

'Yes, of course. If you want.'

If you want.

The worst thing of all is the Look down the table at a dinner party. Luckily the other couples are so busy giving each other their own Looks they're too preoccupied to notice.

'IT'S ALL RIGHT FOR YOU, YOU BASTARD!' I want to scream. 'YOU'VE GOT WILLPOWER!'

I sometimes feel really besieged, backed into a corner by it, as if I'm only one step away from hiding a second bottle of wine in the fridge. Or buying another fridge. But drinking in secret is *worrying*: we all know that, don't we? So I drink openly and put up with the Looks.

I could live with his lack of greed, I suppose, if he only had a vice. He thinks he has. This is his idea of one:

'I do have one of those large bars of chocolate now and then.'

That's like a priest admitting to the odd wank. What use is it, when the rest of the time he's being holier than thou? I once found him — once — secretly scoffing chocolate with his head in the cupboard. And the look on his face when he turned and saw me was quite satisfying. But it didn't last. He didn't go on doing it. So it became all the more memorable for its rarity value. He refers to

17

his occasional lapses with chocolate as if they're proof of an adorable imperfection, thus making him even *more* marvellous, and then carries on having his apple for breakfast and going about like the smug bastard he is.

4

You Have the Right
Not to Remain Silent

Walking along a road near where we live the other day, I saw another couple on the opposite side. The man was wearing glasses which were really far down his nose, as if he was trying to look even older. I nudged Peter, and he said,

'I know what you're thinking: 'Push your glasses up!''

And he was right: I was.

How do you keep it going for the long haul? My friend Mark says the trick is in knowing which characteristics are going to drive you mad in thirty years, but I don't see how you can. For example, whereas ten years ago, when Peter would yawn several times in a row without putting his hand over his mouth, I'd think, 'Tired. Bless!', now I want to smack him.

'The longer you know someone, the more irritating they become,' says my friend John, which is a terrifying thought.

Supposedly, we have a pact to prevent each

other from becoming revolting. In theory, that is. He says,

'You tell me anything I do which revolts you, and I will too.'

And what that means in practice is that I spend half an hour every day smoothing my face and he *promises* to trim his nose hairs. But as they used to say on my therapy course, Trying Doesn't Do It . . .

A couple of years ago I bought him a battery-operated nose-hair trimmer, which he agreed to use, and he knows that I never go for more than twenty-four hours without deploying my tweezers. Of course, with children aged eleven and twelve, whose eyes are like electron microscopes, you don't even need a mirror.

'Your moustache is really noticeable today, Mummy,' they say neutrally, as if remarking upon the weather — which is just as well, since my eyesight isn't what it was. I need to peer into the mirror, but not too close or it all goes blurry, bringing the ever-increasing risk that I will go out looking like an amateur King Lear who's been interrupted halfway through glueing on his false beard. I have to feel the hairs like a dyslexic blind person trying to read a message on my face.

And this isn't just for special occasions. This is every day. I have to spend longer and longer with the tweezers, and the base make-up and the powder, just to get up to zero. We're talking half an hour minimum to reach the level where I can leave the house. Anything on top of that, for example to look *nice*, is another hour. And then it's like alcohol; you need to quit while you're ahead, or you end up like Bette Davis in *Whatever Happened to Baby Jane?* And that, in case you haven't seen it, was a horror film.

But then, even assuming I stop at the right moment, I know I'm lying. I'm saying to the world, 'I look like this' when I don't. I look much, much worse. If you took me out for the evening and then saw me in the morning, you'd think I'd been replaced in the night by my mother — who, yes, is very good-looking, but nonetheless eighty-two.

Also, our entering middle age while the children are still not yet teenagers means the line is now dangerously thin between hilarious observations and those that make your food catch in your throat. And believe me, not everyone is making an equal effort. Whereas I try to maintain some kind of boundary, Peter regards their interest in bodily functions as a licence to drop little nuggets of personal information into the conversation, including, over dinner:

'I think I had the world's longest nose hair

this morning,' he offered recently. 'It was at least 1.5cm.'

'The world record is 12cm,' replied Lawrence. 'And the longest *nipple* hair was 9.4cm.'[1]

'For God's sake, can we just eat our chicken?'

Peter's nipple hair is — well — longer than mine, but since I don't — associate with his nipples, for want of a better phrase, it's not really an issue. God knows we have enough to contend with.

Reflecting upon this after twenty years together, I think what really becomes awful with time is not just the disgusting little things that people do, or sprout, but the fact that they don't notice, or even worse, *do* notice but don't think them worth bothering about.

When I was young, there were still warnings in women's magazines about the dangers of 'letting yourself go', and I can remember a film, from the late fifties, about a wife and mother who gradually gives up on her appearance — and *even the housework* — 'causing' her husband to almost have an affair. It was actually called *Woman in a Dressing Gown*, as if the sheer frightfulness of the image was enough to send moviegoers

---

[1] Thomas Webber, 1821–96, apparently.

shuddering to the box office, like with *The Blob* or *The Creature From the Black Lagoon*.

The husband in the film was played by Anthony Quayle, whose face looked a bit like a bottom. Nowadays she'd have been diagnosed as depressed, due to being stuck indoors for fifteen years with no job or friends and married to a man whose face looked like a bottom. But it was the fifties, and sitting about all day in candlewick and no lipstick was practically tantamount to *forcing* your old man to shag his secretary. And yet there was no corresponding film called *Man in a Vest*, *Man in Slippers*, or, if it had been our marriage, *Man in a Layer of Stubble That Was Quite Cool When He Was Thirty-Five But Now Just Looks as Though His Carers Haven't Turned Up*.

In Peter's favour, and to be fair — though when was that ever any fun? — he has all his hair and no more chins or tummy than when I first met him. He really does look OK. So he can't see what I've got to complain about.

Besides, I've seen enough of other people's husbands to know that I fancy almost none of them and with good reason. It's not just that they tend to go bald and put on weight, but also that they seem to find themselves so — well — acceptable. They don't worry nearly as much about having to please. And no wonder, when we still have the same shocking imbalance. On a website I looked at the other day called Ten Ways to Save Your Marriage, I noticed that number six, 'Take Care of Your Appearance', was aimed *only at women*.

Of course, I know that over a couple of decades it's hard not to let the mystique slip ever so slightly.

I admit that I have been known to eat and talk at the same time. They are my two favourite activities so it's really hard to choose. And there are the occasions — winter being one — when I go to bed in an ensemble of nightie, T-shirt, dressing-gown (flannel, not silk) and, yes, socks. I would argue, however, that if *he* would let *me* have the electric blanket which *I* brought to the marriage, there would be no need for at least three of those. But, no: along with my gorgeous duck-down duvet, it has been consigned to the cupboard under the heading 'likely to cause extreme comfort', and we have to sleep under a duvet like tracing paper, with the window open — no matter what the temperature — huddled into balls.

At least, though, women always wash their hair. If there's one thing which would improve the appeal of most men over fifty, single or married, in my experience, it's more frequent visits to the hairdresser and the shampoo. The other major thing, and I do have to say this, is the compulsion, in company and just anywhere, to pick their noses.

Peter is relatively restrained when it comes to this hideous practice, which makes me wonder why he so frequently fiddles with the end of his nose then rubs his fingers together so it looks as though he's picking it even when he isn't. And in a way that's just as annoying. I can hear it from the other side of the sofa when we're watching television, like the very faint sound of a grasshopper.

I suppose I shouldn't complain. I was in a bar once with a friend, where the tables were really small, and this guy came and sat down right opposite us. And because it was full I didn't feel I could object, even though when you're trying to have an intimate drink with a girlfriend who the hell wants some repulsive stranger sitting two feet away? Obviously I wouldn't have objected if he'd been under fifty and remotely good-looking. Anyhow, he just started picking his nose really blatantly, and there were people eating all around us, so I said, 'Can you not do that, please? It's disgusting.' And he got really aggressive. With my luck in those days, it's a miracle he wasn't my date. Anyway, we left.

Last year sometime, I was walking past an estate agent's one evening and there was a man picking his nose — right in the window. And what really set off the guy in the window was the woman at a nearby desk who either did a very good job of not noticing or really didn't notice: just got on with doing some phoning while he dug away. And since it was a particularly large estate agent's, the huge expanse of glass not only didn't hide it but actually showcased it, as if it were a feature of the service. It was like a little tableau of marriage.

It reminded me, though I've never personally seen them, of those women in stockings and corsets who sit in their front windows in Amsterdam. Actually, that could be how to present male prostitutes for very cautious women, older wives maybe, who don't want anything too different from what they can get at home. They could go to a special section of the red-light district where there are men sitting in windows, picking their noses and reading the paper and not saying anything. You'd pay them, and they'd come round for an hour and carry on doing the same thing. The long-term married in particular I think would jump at it.

5

Stuck in the Lift

Millions of words have been published which seek to help us avoid the mistakes, self-delusions and misjudgements which lead to divorce. But the same conflicts arise, over and over again. And every year, the same divorce lawyers continue to buy themselves summer homes in France. Why?

The Tavi's list tells us at least some of the reasons. But how come the failure rate isn't way higher? Also we argue — quite a lot. And yet we are still married, whereas our friends Judith and Roger, who were far nicer to each other, are not.

So how do some people end up happily married to the most unlikely people?

And:

How the hell does anyone stay married at all?

This book is my attempt to solve these mysteries.

It's also my revenge on Peter for coming over to everyone else as perfect while I express all the anger and frustration in the marriage, causing people to think I'm a bitch. But hey, both goals are valid.

★   ★   ★

When it comes to monogamy, every generation faces a different challenge. For Peter's aunt, the issue was hugely simplified by the fact that the First World War had killed off a lot of the men. She remained single all her life, never left home, and no one thought it was strange. And my grandparents managed to live in the same house long after they no longer loved or even liked each other. Bank managers in the thirties and forties did not get divorced.

My parents met in the mid-fifties, which weren't hugely different. But by the time they ran into trouble, in the sixties, expectations had risen. People thought it reasonable that marriage, and specifically the other person, should make them happier. It wasn't enough to set up home together and, as my father dryly put it, raise a nice little mortgage. There should be fulfilment too. So they separated at a key time, when this basic need was beginning to be seen as the right of women too. I adored my father; he was as involved as a father could be. So I was a bit shocked when my mother told me that he never once got up in the night with us, and indeed on the only occasion she could remember asking him to — I was ill and she had got up three times already — he shouted at her. She was expected to do all that, get up in the morning, make breakfast, get us to school and go to work, as so many women — not me, mind you — still do.

And what do *we* have to worry about? We generally have the children we want, when we want them. We're now entirely conditioned to see happiness and self-expression as our right. Divorce is still hideously painful but no longer shameful. No, for us, the main challenges are to come to terms with the fact that we can't be at work *and* at home, only one *or* the other, and to keep our relationships going for what could be a really, *really* long time.

When you think that the average life expectancy in the UK is between seventy-five and eighty, even if you don't marry too early — say you leave it till around thirty — you're still looking at potentially forty years. That's a *loooooong* time. On the one hand, it's lovely to think of having that one, beloved person by your side until you lose your memory and your teeth fall out. On the other hand, it's also like being stuck in a lift: bearable only so long as someone doesn't reach down and shout through the doors:

'Don't worry! The fire brigade will be here next Tuesday.'

The trick is to get stuck in there with the right person.

But that's not so easy. We have the freedom, but each one of us carries around our own unique tangle of needs, desires, fears, prejudices, insecurities and sexual embarrassments. And when we meet some-one, the likelihood of *their* needs, desires, fears, prejudices, insecurities and sexual embarrassments clashing in some way with ours, or actually exacerbating them, is surely huge. And that's without bringing in all the cultural baggage — the neurotic family patterns and rules of class and community — that we grow up with and most of the time don't even know we're carrying. Twice in the past I've begun — and very quickly ended — relationships with men who were clearly obsessed with their mothers. I mean, when a man turns down sex to put up his mother's shelves, it is a bit of a warning sign. On the other hand, maybe he'd gone off me over lunch.

In this culture, we're very keen on *The One*, as if love were a treasure hunt. Go through the maze, find the Right Man — or Woman — and live happily ever after. Some of us seek to protect ourselves from making a mistake by having a fixed idea of the sort of person we think we want, like a style of kitchen design, and trying to find them. And, as with designing kitchens, it's a teensy bit more complicated than it first seems.

6

The Belt and Braces Approach

I was in my mid-twenties when I began to think seriously about my emotional future, i.e. that I was in danger of not having one. I was a journalist with a passionate interest in jazz and R&B music. I also loved eating out and going to the cinema. So I looked for someone else who did too. It made perfect sense.

Except that it didn't. The two main relationships I had before Peter were with music journalists who liked going to the cinema. Robert ticked pretty much all the boxes — funny, creative, intelligent, film-mad, and, though vegetarian, an excellent cook. We spent most of the relationship lying in bed eating and watching old films. And in between the food and films, the sex was great. It all blew up after a surprisingly short time, though, when he decided he didn't want to see me any more. But he didn't tell me that. For the final four weeks of it, I stuck it out with virtually no communication except monosyllabic sulks, until one night I rang him and got him to admit that he had chucked me. I got over it, but I do think you should let a person know.

Phil was a lovely man who also seemed right on the surface of it, but we found we didn't want the same things out of life. For example, my ambition was to get a book on the bestseller list, while he wanted to go round Ghana on a motorbike. We just didn't match. I spent months hoping he would let me down in some way so I could end it, but he was too nice. So I accidentally slept with two other people — I mean, without deliberately setting out to, and not at the same time — but almost as if to make him end it; what you might call the belt and braces approach. He found out, and it was over. To his credit we are still in touch, and I do hope that he will find the right woman because decent, forty-something men with good taste in music, and who are good with children, shouldn't go to waste.

Yet even after those two experiences had suggested rather clearly that it didn't work, I totally failed to learn the obvious lesson and continued to blunder on, looking for someone 'compatible'.

Peter was therefore on the face of it the wrong choice. My ideal man was big and hairy-chested and he was thin with even less chest hair than me. Nor did he fulfil the requirement to be good in the kitchen. In fact, being good in the kitchen was almost more important than being good in the bedroom. My fantasies began with a man in a stripy apron making me dinner and mostly ended with pudding. And Peter didn't cook at all. Well, he did — once. He made chicken casserole. Then I slept with him, and he never did it again.

But that wasn't even the worst of it. He claimed not to like jazz or R&B, preferring the warblings of female vocalists who sounded very delicate, like those girls who were always being kept off school by their mothers for just a sniffle. The gutsier ones weren't my type either; I even spotted a *country* album in his collection. My early attempt to educate him, a concert by the great pianist Horace Silver at Ronnie Scott's, ended with his falling asleep in the middle of it.

Going to the cinema at least wasn't a problem, except that our first proper date together was to see a so-called comedy horror which I left in the middle. And when we began spending weekends together, I discovered more counts against him. His idea of a nice Sunday was to go for a long, muddy walk — in itself unappealing enough — with no pub lunch at the end of it. Then what was the big 'treat' when we got back? Formula One on television and a bowl of pasta. Not even with bolognese! And I didn't discover how many model cars he owned until after we were married. When he said he had 'a few things in storage', I assumed he meant books and furniture, like normal people.

7

The C Word

So how did I get involved with someone so wrong and yet so right, but so very annoying?

I was coming up to thirty, and you could say I'd made progress. I'd moved on from men to whom Commitment meant staying the night afterwards, or who lived a bit far away — for example in New York. And I'd managed to graduate to the likes of Phil: more local, nice even, but unfortunately all wrong for me. It was forward momentum, but of an almost imperceptible kind, like leaving dead plant matter in the ground and waiting for it to turn into coal. At this rate, I'd be in the right relationship by the time I was about 103.

I couldn't even complain, like nuns or manicurists, that I never met any men. I met plenty. They just all seemed to be *either* on the same mental wave-length *or* kind and attentive, never both. I wanted one who was gentle *and* exciting, who would take me to cool places but then not suddenly vanish when I suggested he meet my dad.

And even when I did meet men who

vaguely matched this description, they never chose me. So I had to start asking myself, was it really just down to sheer bad luck? For a mere coincidence it did seem to happen an awful lot. Put me in a pub, a club or a private view in a gallery, the result was the same: I would ruin it — maybe not on the first night, maybe not on the second, but sooner rather than later. Sometimes I could even ruin it in the first paragraph. I'd concentrate so hard on not being Intense I'd go too far the other way, and cover my terror with a kind of defensive flirting that may just *possibly* have been a bit much. Up in that attic bit of the mind where everything works perfectly, I was modelling myself on the wisecracking hero-ines of the Hollywood golden age, who delivered drop-dead hilarious ripostes while sashaying across the room in flared satin and high heels. Looking back on it, I probably sounded like Belle Watling, the eye-rolling brothel keeper in *Gone With the Wind*.

I tried to appear normal but I was faking and it showed. Most shaming of all, I was already in therapy. Not the quickest or cheapest strategy, you may think, but when I considered the alternatives — drugs, suicide, religion — believe me, sitting in a room with a guy who didn't say very much was the least hideous option. And at least the room was warm.

'Why don't you choose your boyfriends the way you choose your girlfriends?' said my mother, who to her credit had never said, 'Why don't you try going out with blokes who aren't married, a bit sinister or thick?'

'What do *you* know?' I said.

One night, Polly, a friend of my mother's from the country, took my sister Claire and me out for supper. At seventy she still fizzed with an infectious manic energy, and when she got bored with greenery would rush up to London for fixes of culture and urban stress. At about ten p.m., just as we were having pudding, she suddenly said,

'Hey, why don't we have coffee with my friend Pete? He lives near here.'

'What, now?'

Claire and I looked at each other. What kind of bloke would be in, expecting a call from an ancient female? Someone equally ancient, but knowing Polly, interesting. We decided to go along with it. Besides, before we could protest, she had jumped up and was on her way to the payphone.

Claire said, 'What's she up to?'

'Dunno,' I said. 'It's a bit weird, if you ask me.'

'Well, if he's over sixty you can have him.'

'Cheers very much.'

She was already living with someone, which since she was my younger sister only served to heighten my sense of inadequacy.

Peter's flat was tidy and welcoming, though I couldn't help noticing he had the front of an old car in his fireplace, as if it had been driven through from the house next door: a 1939 Chrysler, he later explained, as if that somehow made it more normal. Also, for some reason, though he did have furniture, he was sitting on the floor. Was he into yoga, or some kind of alternative belief system? But maybe I could overlook that. He was thirty-two and worked at the BBC: attractive, interesting and way out of my league. He invited me to lunch a couple of days later and said,

'I was a bit surprised when you two showed up at my flat the other night.'

'Why?'

'When Polly said she was bringing along two 'girls' I thought she meant two old dears.'

So I had exceeded his expectations merely by walking without a stick. I just had to make sure he didn't find out I was a manic-depressive with moth-eaten carpets, a hole in her sitting room wall and her former stepmother still living upstairs.

Lunch was in a nice restaurant, so even if the relationship didn't get off the ground at least I would have eaten well. And the fact that he was a BBC producer would impress my father. Peter told me about a new programme he was working on, about youth culture — the latest cutting-edge trend — and he brought me back to the office to meet his co-producer. I'd been doing some TV auditions, so this got my hopes up. He was clearly thinking of giving me a job. He said he would be in touch and I went home and wrote him a letter to say thank you for the lunch, and to express my tremendous enthusiasm for his brilliant youth culture series.

But I didn't hear from him. So I rang his office to suggest another lunch. He wasn't there. I left a message and when I heard nothing, rang a second time. A man who managed to sound both flirtatious and off-hand took the message.

'Um, can you just ask him if he wants to come to lunch this Sunday?'

My sister was cooking. There'd be other people. It wasn't intense.

'Sure,' said the man. 'It sounds good. I'd go.'

I nearly asked him. After all, it was only lunch. I waited a couple of days: nothing. Then a week. Still nothing.

'Well, if he's playing Hard To Get he's very good at it,' said Dad.

★   ★   ★

Two years later, he rang me back.

40

8

Heads, Bodies and Legs

I thought of pretending not to remember him but I've always been useless at deception; I think people can read my mind, as a result of which they usually can. Besides, I knew he'd seen Polly recently, so she'd surely told him to call, probably told him my latest relationship had just ended — no surprise there — and why didn't he do me a favour and take me out?

I wasn't going to make it easy for him.

'I did get your message that time,' he began.

'Oh, really?'

Who do these people think they are?

'Yeah. I'm sorry I didn't ring you back. I thought you were great.'

'Really.'

Yeah, right. Don't patronize me, you bloody — telly person.

'The thing was, I'd just started seeing someone and — I didn't want to complicate things.'

Yeah? Feel free to tell me next time.

41

Anyhow, who cares? I don't fancy you. Your face is too long, so there.

'Fine. That's — understandable.'

'I was wondering if you're free for dinner this week?'

Fuck off: I'm not that desperate.

'That'd be lovely.'

Lunch, and two years later, dinner. For someone with my fear of commitment he had actually got it about right.

After dinner he drove me home, in a strangely shaped twenty-year-old Citroën that, when he switched on the ignition, rose on its wheels. We had coffee at my place and talked for four hours, during which all my inadequacies seemed to melt away. This was a huge improvement on men I'd known in the past for whom the word 'coffee' acted as a remote control on their trouser zips, or the ones for whom coffee did just mean coffee because they had absolutely no conversation, so, knowing they'd leave immediately afterwards, you ended up having sex with them just to get them out of the house.

Finally, at about three a.m., we came to say goodbye. We stood for a while in the open doorway, then he kissed me on the lips. Thinking the next one would probably be with tongues, I closed my eyes, only to see him disappear out of the door, leaving me, head craned forward and lips puckered, like Tom in *Tom and Jerry*, thinking he's about to be romanced by a female cat who is in fact Jerry standing on a mop with a gun up his blouse instead.

A few days later we went to the cinema, to see the film which was meant to be a horror spoof, and which wasn't either scary or funny. After about half an hour I turned to him and whispered, 'I'm not madly keen on this, to be honest. Do you mind if we go?' thinking he'd leap to his feet.

Instead, he said, 'Actually I'm quite enjoying it.'

Fair enough, I suppose, but I couldn't stick another minute. I hung around in the lobby till it was due to end, then realized with a jolt that thanks to my cinematic fussiness, he might have written the whole thing off and gone home. If a man had gone off me, I didn't like to be told twice. I went outside, and was on my last linger, just about to head for the bus stop, when I saw him by one of the side exits behind Piccadilly.

'Sorry,' I said. 'I just thought it was a bit rubbish.'

'Actually so did I,' he admitted. 'I just didn't like to leave.'

Hmm! Perhaps we could make a go of it after all.

However, our next date didn't start off too brilliantly either. He took me to a party. Everyone else there was from his office and all they wanted to talk about was work. I was so bored that eventually, just for something to do, I went to the bathroom. I sat down gratefully on the loo and after what must only have been a few minutes, was startled by a strange, falling sensation which I suddenly realized was me waking up.

This'll be the clincher, I thought. If he makes me stay here, listening to his workmates moaning about their terms of employment, that's it. It's easy to forget how precarious the early months of a relationship can be. At that stage, even quite minor irritations or differences can scupper it. After all, we'd just met, I had no big investment in it, so why shouldn't I be fussy? I was still the right side of thirty and by no means desperate to settle down and have children. It certainly wasn't one of those situations where the relationship is rubbish but you're in your thirties and you've already put in a couple years, so keep it going even though you don't want to, like a really horrible flat you want to leave but you've just put in new floors.

To my relief he said,

'Yeah, I've had enough too. Shall we go and get something to eat?'

This'll be good, I thought: a wine bar or perhaps an atmospheric bistro, somewhere intimate and not too well lit.

He took me to Dalston, an area of north London I knew as the fault line between the gentrified avenues of Islington and Hackney's notorious 'Murder Mile'. I had once been to a nightclub there when I worked for a listings magazine, a nightclub where you couldn't see across the room for the cannabis smoke and which closed down after one of the owners was shot. At the time I was mildly thrilled by the edginess of it all. Now I was looking for something ever so slightly safer. And just as I thought life was leading me away from all that, I was back. I had this effect on men; even the high-powered ones immediately lowered their standards when they met me. Even when I was a young reporter, when a big tabloid editor invited me out for a drink, it was at a dingy drinking den with torn seats because he, with his huge expense account, was 'bored' with the American Bar at the Savoy. I wanted to be spoiled a bit, or at least for the evening not to end with someone falling over or having to call the police.

Peter pulled up in a quiet residential road and gestured at a brightly lit shopfront. It was now about eleven p.m.

'Welcome to the Ridley Road 24-Hour

45

Bagel Bakery,' he said.

We got our bagels, still warm from the enormous oven, and ate them in the car, watching the customers come and go. Several were black guys with dreadlocks in those wide Jaguar XK6s. The strange combination of the people, the cars and the food seemed incongruous and dreamlike: an urban, night-time version of Heads, Bodies and Legs.

'I thought only posh businessmen drove Jags,' I said.

'Not really. You can pick one up for about eight grand.'

'*Really?*'

I'd never been interested in the demo-graphics of car ownership before, but this was fascinating. I wanted to hear more. And I realized also that I no longer wanted to be in a wine bar or at the Savoy. Having supper in a paper bag, with this thin man in his strange up-and-down car, was where I wanted to be. So I had to make sure I didn't ruin it by sleeping with him.

Like a lot of hopeless cases, I was convinced that the main reason most of my relationships went wrong was because I had sex with men too soon, and they stopped respecting me. Before that point, I believed, was a golden period during which everything went right. This was of course complete rubbish, based on the dubious evidence of several doomed flings with men who didn't respect me even before we had sex and never would have done, even if I'd held out till the menopause. Nonetheless, I clung to the idea because it was the one area over which I believed I had a bit of control. I wasn't accomplished enough to hide the major defects in my personality; I could, however, just about manage to keep my clothes on for a couple of weeks.

Peter drove me home, and invited me to supper early the following week; he was going to cook.

Clearly this was too good to be true. I felt my stomach muscles tightening, a sure sign that I had met The One. Probably. Maybe. Definitely. What I must do was try very hard not to fuck it up.

Then another thought occurred to me. He hadn't made any attempt to have sex with me yet. I'd thought this was charming, but what if I was wrong? Maybe he was putting it off too. After all, I'd worked in the music business; I was used to men whose idea of leaving it a while was to wait until the tour bus got back to the hotel. Maybe he had something wrong with him, or was so awful in bed he was trying to delay the moment until I had been captivated by his personality and it was too late. The more I thought about it, there was bound to be a flaw — somewhere. People like me simply did not end up with men like this. Either that or men who seemed like this weren't really like this and were actually married or insane.

The best I could reasonably hope for was either someone creative and sexy but horrible and mad, or sweet but dull: never the best of both. In the meantime, whatever the outcome, I should just get on with the date. This was my chance to have a proper look at his flat, so at worst, it could be my opportunity to find the catch, whatever it was, and then go back to my life. At the very least I would get supper.

★ ★ ★

I arrived to be greeted by a promising aroma of chicken. There was a cat litter tray in the kitchen, but the smell of chicken was definitely coming from the cooker. The last guy I'd dated who'd had a cat kept its tray in the kitchen and the smell caught my throat whenever I went in there. (The relationship ended after it dawned on me that he was travelling home miles across north London to feed it, rather than spend the nights with me.)

Peter's flat not only smelled a great deal

nicer but also had French windows and a garden front and back. And it was an actual garden, not a yard with half a bike and an old sink. There was even a wisteria, climbing up the front stairs. The interior was clean, but not suggestive of obsessive-compulsive disorder, and furnished with a normal degree of blokishness. Grey featured heavily — it was very in then — but unlike my place, also big on the grey, it didn't look like an abandoned stationery office. I flicked through his LPs: Blondie, Talking Heads and the B52s. Hmm, and a Crystal Gayle. I didn't like any of them particularly, but at least they were good.

I'd walked from the station in trainers, so I went into the bedroom to put on my heels. One entire wall was lined with books: ooh. But they looked unfamiliar.

I settled my eyes on a shelf at random: *The Decline of British Industry* — and next to it, *Labour in Power: 1945-51*.

Uh-oh . . .

I went down a shelf: *History of British Dinky Toys* . . . *The Power of Steam* . . . *Toyota: Fifty Years in Motion* . . . *Rover P6-1963-1977*.

Was this the catch? Or was there something worse?

I went up a shelf:

Kurt Vonnegut, Saul Bellow, William

Faulkner, Zola, Ibsen, Beckett and Thomas Mann. He was a nerd *and* an intellectual: well done, Steph.

I'd tried to read *Slaughterhouse Five* once, and had got to page two. And that was a struggle. As for Faulkner, zero. My sister had done a bit of Faulkner at university; she was the educated one. Maybe I should call her and, like Cyrano de Bergerac, she could stand outside the window and prompt.

Anyhow, I couldn't hide in the bedroom all night. I edged towards the door, and noticed something odd leaning against *The Boys' Book of Buses of the World*: a beer mat bearing the caption 'Don't just stand there, do something!' I turned it over: a groovy young girl in a 1960s minidress stood pointing provocatively beside the second part of the message: 'Become a Young Conservative!' I'd steer the conversation round towards that. At least then I could say I'd read something on the shelves.

On the stereo he had the Gipsy Kings, the coolest sound of the moment. He served the chicken, and I really wished I had done an English degree. On the other hand, with all those books about cars and buses on his shelves he probably *was* terrible in bed. On the *other* hand, he had cooked. And when he was cooking, and the conversation got animated, he turned away from the stove every now and then to gesture with his spatula in the most adorable way.

'You've got great taste in beer mats,' I said.

'Yeah,' he said. 'If there's ever a fire, I'm definitely going to save that.'

He cleared the plates away and scraped them before he stacked, but not too neatly. We moved to the sofa. He didn't talk about model cars, the first fifty years of Toyota or the Rover P6. It was going quite well. Then he made a passing reference to Saul Bellow.

And I felt my confidence just dribble away.

I could try to keep him off politics, history and literature for an evening, but not for ever. What, did I think I could carry on changing the subject indefinitely? Then be found out, twenty years on, when we had a mortgage and two kids? Like those people who spend their whole lives saying they can't find their glasses whenever they have to pay a bill or look up the TV listings because they never learned to read? Why didn't I just get it over with? I picked at the end of the sofa arm, which was oddly shredded.

'The cats,' he said. I had seen the two black kittens and even though I didn't really like animals, thought them rather cute.

'Look,' I said finally. 'There's something you should know about me. Something you

51

might not — like.'

We were sitting quite close to each other now. He looked slightly unnerved, but prepared.

'I'm listening.'

'Well. The thing is. It could be a problem — in the future.'

'You're scaring me now. Spit it out.'

'I haven't read any Saul Bellow. Or — any of them in there.'

'Is that it? Oh my God!'

He said afterwards he thought I was going to tell him I had herpes.

When he'd stopped laughing he kissed me, and I shut my eyes.

'Mm, can I stay?' I said.

Then I fell asleep.

He gave me a T-shirt to wear, and most of his bed, where I snuggled down comfortably. He didn't look sleepy at all.

When I woke up the next morning, it was *warm*. He had central heating. Ooh yes, I thought: he really might be The One.

We had toast and coffee at a table in the small back garden. Suddenly, we heard the loud rumble of a lorry, which jolted us from our weekday-morning reverie.

'You know what that is?' he said. 'It's the Toast Detector Van. It comes round with an antenna that picks up who's eating toast, so it knows you're not at work. And if it catches you, it takes you away.'

So we stayed very quiet with our lips pressed together just as Tilly and I used to at school, when we'd pushed our luck too far and been sent to sit outside the Head's office.

As I sipped my coffee — in a rather smart blue-and-white French cup, with a saucer — I could feel my resistance starting to break down. He was clever, funny, successful and had a really warm flat: either I'd finally hit the jackpot or something was about to go spectacularly wrong.

9

Incompatibly Yours

This was starting to feel scarily like a relationship. But I was still horribly uncertain — of him and myself. I couldn't just — let it happen. It *was* happening. But I still felt there *must* be a catch. One night I asked him,

'If you're so wonderful, how come you're not married?'

'I just haven't met the right woman.'

'Oh, come on!' I Paxmanned.

He was thirty-five. After years of believing any old rubbish from men — 'My phone's not working'/ 'We're still married but I'm moving out any day now'/'I can't call you more than once a month: I work on an oil rig' — I was experimenting with a new technique: finding a nice man and attempting to put him off.

We reached Christmas Eve, the day before our first Christmas together, which we were going to be spending with a friend of mine who was divorced and, more to the point, a fantastic cook. With a judicious blend of white lies — 'Can't leave poor divorced friend on her own,' etc. (she had her children and about ten friends coming) — I had got myself a pass off seeing my parents. This meant I could avoid — and more importantly avoid letting Peter experience — the hideous cat's cradle of my mother, my father and his girlfriend, which I thought would quite possibly kill off the relationship there and then. So I was already playing truant from my life.

It was one of those twilight English mornings when you could be forgiven for putting brandy in your coffee because you feel it will never get properly light. We left Peter's flat and went shopping, for tangerines and tea bags and tinsel and washing-up liquid, like people who — I could hardly breathe the thought — *lived together.* Was he noticing this too? Was I the only one thinking, '*We look like two people walking normally down the road but we're sliding into domesticity here . . . and it feels wonderful — aaaaaargh!*'? I didn't dare complete the thought.

We walked through the market, the old, traditional sort where you get twenty oranges for a pound and flashing clockwork toys and those multipacks of Imperial Leather soap. And floating across the grey skies, behind the calls of '*Get your wrapping paper here, ladies! Ten sheets a pound!*', we heard music: happy, sunny music. We quickened our pace, and there among the sprouts and cheap scarves and packs of batteries, an African record stall materialized out of the gloom. It was almost like a mirage, something you might hallucinate if stuck out at sea or the edge of the Arctic Circle. Also, in all the years I'd known it, this market had never had any black traders before. So it felt to me like Fate. 'Something unprecedented is happening,' the universe seemed to be telling me. 'Take that step into the unknown!'

We bought the album that was playing.[1] We didn't literally pool our money, but without explicitly saying so, and several years before we finally did move in together, we were expressing an intention to end up sharing a stereo. Nowadays, with everybody file-sharing and swapping iPods all over the place, this might not seem hugely significant but we were the last generation to have only one music system per household, so it was a gesture of massive proportions, probably equivalent in today's terms to buying a car. We took it back to his place, hung up the tinsel and danced. All we'd done was buy an LP on a cold, grey morning, and yet I felt fantastic.

---

[1] By the Congolese artist Evvi Rochereau, if you're curious, and it still sounds great.

10

We'll Always Have Bologna

I had been so good at giving men space and not scaring them off that when they didn't turn up for a date, or didn't give me a birthday present, or avoided meeting my family — a teensy clue that someone is probably not anticipating a shared future — I'd pretend I didn't mind. So going on holiday with them was *way* out of reach. The only romantic holiday I had managed before was a week in France with Michael, whose family had a dark farmhouse with no pool. It rained most of the time, he didn't want to go anywhere — chateaux, restaurants, the nearest village — and I realized by the end of the first day that I'd made a hideous mistake. All I had for entertainment was a copy of *The Silence of the Lambs*, and when you prefer the company of Hannibal Lecter, even at dinner, you know you're with the wrong man.

So I was surprised when I heard myself agreeing to go on holiday with Peter, amazed when he didn't change his mind or come to his senses, and astonished when I actually found myself on the plane.

We went to Italy, where his fear of languages and my inability to choose which clothes to bring turned out to have an unexpected upside. Due no doubt to the early trauma of putting my things in a case every week to leave my mother for my father, I had just a touch of neurosis related to the area of packing.

'Rubbish,' said Peter later, without a hint of sympathy. 'You just can't finish anything.'

(Hmm. As I write this, I am acutely aware of the half-made Christmas pudding in the kitchen, which I really could finish before he gets back to spare myself one of his Looks, yet almost certainly won't.)

I could put the things in the case; I just couldn't complete. He had to come along afterwards like a surgeon and close it all up. And the prospect of repeating the process every day or two as we hopped from one pensione to another defeated me completely. He did it all — and without accidentally desegregating. To maintain my separateness, and in case it all went wrong, I resolutely kept my stuff separate from his. On the third or fourth night, I realized I had left a favourite top behind in our previous pensione — and he went back to get it. It ended up in his case for a night, and I tried not to overreact, for example by letting out a yelp.

'My top is in your case,' I said, and immediately regretted it; now he would definitely know I was weird.

'Ha,' he replied. 'Our luggage has mingled. You can't escape now!'

What a relief. He'd managed to zero in on my neurosis and take the piss out of it while at the same time making me feel less of a freak. It felt strange but good, a bit like shedding a skin: at first the new skin tingled slightly, but without the old one I could now grow to the next stage.

My contribution was to do all the talking, asking and ordering. With my uninhibited volleys of verbs and tenses — 'A room, the bed very big. You had?' — we didn't once have to sleep in the car. And if I rejected a room as being too brown or having sad wallpaper, which on our budget was reasonably likely, he didn't say, 'I'm a heterosexual man: we don't care if the wallpaper is sad.'

And he *ironed*. In Cortona, I watched him manoeuvre a side table into a doorway to enable his travel iron to reach the socket, so we could go to dinner in uncreased clothes. Then I thought: no one will believe this. So I photographed it.

In San Sepolcro, the birthplace of Piero della Francesca, we went to the museum to see the great artist's paintings of angels. After about two dozen, I was deeply bored. But we couldn't just walk out; it would look bad. Besides, I was the daughter of artists; I was supposed to be into this stuff. But I sensed he wasn't exactly riveted either. I left it a few minutes then said,

'Did you notice that café just back there . . . ?'

Uh oh, I thought. I've just revealed how shallow I am. I mean, leaving an exhibition before you've been all the way round it — that's just not allowed.

'Come on,' he said. 'Let's go and have coffee.'

'Really? Again?'

'We're on holiday!'

It felt as good as bunking off games to go to the cake shop with Tilly, except that with him I could have sex as well.

Towards the end of the trip, we booked in at a faded old villa, where the shutters on our windows hung ever so romantically off their hinges. We went out for dinner and afterwards he said,

'Come on, let's go for a drive.'

We drove west towards Pisa and after a while saw an urban skyline: the usual Renaissance church tops mingled with more recent, squarer shapes.

'Do you notice anything strange?' he said.

'No, what? Oh my God . . . '

Sticking out above the roofline was something quite bizarre. It pointed up diagonally at a really strange angle, like a huge white cannon aimed at the sky. I recognized it immediately. But it was far more beautiful and more extraordinary than I'd imagined: the Leaning Tower, bathed in white light. In my memory, of course, it's moonlight, though I know there were spotlights round it. Peter had seen it before, yet I felt that he too was experiencing this wondrous creation for the first time: so stunning and yet so *odd*. The fact that it was still standing against all expectations I felt was another Sign: I should attempt the impossible, too.

We drove back all aglow and in the morning set off for our next stop: Maranello, near Modena, the home of Ferrari. We were going to look round the museum there, which he assured me would be fascinating and not at all dull. And he was right; he had already got so far under my skin that I, who until five minutes ago hadn't known the difference between a Dino 246 and a 308 — imagine! — was going to spend a day looking at *cars*. This was very foreign.

That evening we missed dinner, and after

several futile circuits of Bologna's one-way system, failed to reach the nice-sounding hotel I'd efficiently booked on the phone. We'd have to find somewhere else. Also, I'd managed to use two verbs correctly in the same sentence when booking, and it was annoying to see it go to waste.

Tired and hungry, we dumped the car, booked ourselves into a grim, dark pensione, and went out to try to find the sweet-looking little restaurant I'd glimpsed as we whizzed round the one-way system. It seemed to have vanished, so we came back again to find another place that wasn't quite as nice, and looked full, but might have a table by now. And by the time we got back there they had plenty of tables because they were closed. So we stood in the street and yelled at each other, in true Italian style, like two *mammas* in a tenement. It exhausted both of us and when he stormed off, leaving me there, I really thought it possible he had gone to the airport and flown home. But I was hungry and that had to take priority. After all, I could probably get another boyfriend, but my stomach needed filling *now*. Anyhow, better surely to break up now than in the future, when we had kids.

I turned a couple of corners and found a bar. By some piece of luck it wasn't populated by three old men staring into space, but by friendly, understanding females who poured me prosecco, toasted me a sandwich and agreed between them that whoever had got me into this state was unquestionably *stronso*. I looked this up later as it was not in my pocket Italian dictionary; it's not a word you could use in front of your mother-in-law.

I had a lovely time, and when I returned to our room two hours later with a ham and cheese croissant wrapped in a napkin, a hand reached out from under the blanket in a gesture of conciliation. And I handed over the croissant, and then his face appeared too, and we kissed. I'd never had a row with a man before, apart from my dad. I didn't know that you *could* have one and not break up for good.

Quite a few years later, we were watching *Casablanca* together. At the moment where Humphrey Bogart is trying to persuade Ingrid Bergman to get on the plane and leave him, and she doesn't want to, he says — as you may remember:

'We'll always have Paris.'

And Peter turned to me and said:

'We'll always have Bologna.'

Not Pisa.

And I felt this huge surge of love.

11

The Looming Towers of Pyrex

We'd had our first big argument and survived. And, I realized, once we were back in London, I was in love. Even better, so was he — with me!

Both his parents were dead, so as proof of his honourable intentions he took me to visit his stepmother. Or rather, he brought me to his place of origin to show me that although I was from Bloomsbury and he was from Sheffield, though the view from the end of his road was of the Peak District and mine was of a pub and a chip shop, he *understood*.

He too had had a dad who'd married another woman. That his mother was dead, and not living on the floor below like mine, didn't make it any easier. Though his father had managed fine for five years, once she was installed, Beryl was determined to carry out her wifely duties to the full. Out went the light, fluffy omelettes and salads his father had taught himself to make; in came the dense slabs of meat, clean shirts for dinner and Father's Chair. It was, he said, like going back in time.

'She'd been an ex-pat all her working life. And while she was away the Sixties happened and everything changed.'

Beryl preferred things as they had been. She was a tireless toiler for those less fortunate, a rescuer of foreign babies from floods and earthquakes, and a properly trained nurse. Oddly enough, when she met the children of Lawrence Grimsdale, she wasn't quite so enamoured of them. It seemed their proximity may have been the problem, being in the home of her beloved rather than in the Gambia or Bangladesh.

His father adored her. And just before I met Peter, he died, leaving her behind like an unwanted bequest. No one in the family seemed very keen on her, but I wasn't daunted. I was an expert in these matters.

'Don't talk to me about stepmothers,' I told him. 'I've had them up to here.'

Technically, my dad had only actually remarried the once, but over the years we'd seen a colourful parade of women — mostly either dim and gorgeous or clever and complicated, and the current one was married to someone else.

'I'm prepared for anything,' I said. 'You may have one of Britain's premier National

Parks on your doorstep, but have you cleared up the glass after the lovelorn parent's put his hand through a window?'

He countered this by suggesting we get married.

'Married! Here we are going to see your stepmother — proof that love doesn't last — and you ask me that?!'

So he can't say he wasn't warned.

Beryl still lived in Peter's childhood home in Ecclesall, the nice part of Sheffield, where she had amassed a vast collection of knick-knacks from her various postings around the world, and many towers of Pyrex. When she opened the kitchen cupboards they loomed out at us, daring me to be a better home-maker. There was still quite a lot of the jam she'd made for his father in the larder.

'It sounds very impressive,' I said, as we drank tea on abnormally upright wing-back chairs. 'Your work for Save the Children.'

'Not really,' she said. 'Why?'

'Well!' I said. 'Dinner smells delicious!'

She gave a small, tightly rationed laugh.

'I shouldn't think so. Why do you say that?'

And on it went, for thirty-six excruciating hours. I had never been so polite to someone with so little result. Still, it made an interesting contrast from dealing with my own stepmother, who was far better at conversation but had recently conked out with a cigarette, or something, in her hand, and set her flat on fire.

That night Peter and I lay giggling on our sides facing each other in his old single bed, under a shelf of bound issues of *Meccano* magazine — 1961-66, and had cramped, trying-to-be-quiet sex. I didn't feel the ambience was quite conducive, but he seemed to want to make some kind of statement and I didn't want to get in his way.

On the Sunday morning, after I watched her lowering a helpless joint of beef into a pan of butter, I said to him,

'I think she's going to raise your cholesterol high enough to kill you so she won't have to leave you the house.'

'Well,' he said, 'we could take her up to Stanage Edge and give her a shove.'

While she was safely occupied in the kitchen — she treated all offers of help as if I believed she wasn't up to the job — he took me into the front room.

'There's something I want to show you.'

Aha! What was it going to be? A portrait of a renegade, dodgy uncle? A piece of jewellery of his mother's? He knelt down and unhooked the front of a low, long cupboard in the front room. It unfolded several times and in several directions, like a huge board

67

game: it was an enormous model railway.

'My father made this,' he said. 'All of it, including the case.'

What a relief. I had found the catch at last. He might later bring it down to London and invite me to lie naked in the middle of it while the four-fifteen to Preston tootled round me, but it was a risk I was prepared to take. Besides, there were worse things to share a house with: most of the men I'd ever known, for a start.

We took the slow route home, and talked about our families.

'So,' I said, 'anyone else I should see before I commit myself?'

'You know what, though? They were really happy together.'

My parents — my talented, funny, inventive parents — couldn't stay married, but his father and Beryl did. How did he square it with his memories of his mother?

'They're just so different,' he said thoughtfully. 'He was much younger when he married Mum, at the start of the war.'

Like so many couples then, they were kept apart for several years and the children — first his sisters, then he — were born after quite long gaps.

'And were *they* happy together?'

'I think so. They never seemed *unhappy*. I

68

know he loved travelling though, and Mum didn't.'

'And Beryl did?'

'Loved it. She's very intrepid.'

There were enough boots and Gore-tex in the hall cupboard to clothe a battalion. And that wasn't all; from mountains to malarial swamps, Beryl would go anywhere, and she never failed to uphold the traditional British values of speaking loudly and clearly, and serving a roast Sunday lunch.

I tried to make sense of it, but mysterious forces were at work in these matters, impossible to harness and control. Maybe marriage was like Frankenstein's Creature: you put the parts together, fired electricity into it, and couldn't predict if it would play nicely or rampage through the village trampling all in its path.

On the last stretch of the journey, passing through north London, we passed a pub with a ridiculous name. Various harmless old boozers called the Horse's Head or the Queen's Bloomers had been replaced by a chain called the Fox and Firkin.

'I bet you also hate the word *firkin*,' said Peter.

And I thought: yes, I probably could live with this man.

12

I'm Afraid It's Serious

'I think this is it,' I told my friends, my mother, my father, the girl who zapped my chin hairs and anyone else who couldn't get away. 'As in *It*.'

'So it's Serious?' said Dad, in the same way you might respond to news of a life-threatening condition, which in a way it was. For Peter was about to overturn everything I held dear, from my stubbornly preserved loneliness to my unheated, tumbledown flat.

We went out for dinner, and having softened me up with claret and steak and chips, he suggested we try living together.

'Oh yes!' I said. 'You want me to give up my cheap, convenient flat, move in with you, get pregnant and just — lose everything!'

'I hadn't thought that far ahead, to be honest. I just thought it might be nice.'

'Nice? *Nice?!* You just want to take away my independence! And I'll end up divorced with two children like my mother!'

In my head I saw my nightmare vision: a washing machine, with me and two children

70

trapped in a room with it — which was weird, because I'd only recently got a washing machine and I worshipped it. As for my mother, she did hardly any housework, and my father took more interest in his kids than most men who were still there. She was hardly an oppressed single mother.

'Why would I move, though?'

'You said yourself the flat is cold and leaky.'

It was freezing. There was an actual hole in the sitting-room wall where the rain came in, and, more recently, snow.

'Now you've nailed that piece of hardboard up it's fine.'

'And there's the pub opposite, and the common parts are never cleaned.'

He was right. I was fed up with coming home to find people being sick in the doorway, and having to step over litter and spilled drinks on the stairs. The landlords had long since stopped cleaning the building, the uncollected post of myriad past tenants was strewn across the landings, and the ones who remained liked to party. Sometimes there was more alcohol being consumed in my building than in the pub. And we only had five flats.

My sister, my *younger* sister, had gone to live with her boyfriend, in a nice, normal flat which they had done up to look really good. When I moved a chest of drawers in her old room I found that an entire corner of the carpet had been eaten by moths. And while my father was at least no longer living on the floor above, his ex-wife, my ex-stepmother, was. I tried not to let people find out about the last bit, but when they did, I could see them looking at me differently, as if I was either mad, or had made it up.

'It's cheap, and I can walk to the best cake shop in London,' I said.

Had I put him off? Was this going to be the moment when he gave up?

'You could still get to the cake shop,' he said. 'I just think we would make each other happy.'

Looking back, it's almost as if he knew what was best for me even then, and this was just the first in a long line of decisions — marrying, having children, moving to a nice, leafy area without people being sick in the doorways — that, left to myself, I could never have made. But I was like someone in a burning plane with a parachute who just won't jump — even though the parachute itself was making a really good case.

Poor Peter. I really do feel a bit sorry about all that. But the thought of marrying and — by implication — having children was just terrifying. It would be bound to go wrong and I would end up worse off than before. At least when you're alone and miserable you're used to it. Let myself get dependent on someone, allow myself to *need* them, and I'd be setting myself up for rejection, abandonment *and* the loss of my pride. I didn't need years of therapy to tell me this, though I was having them anyway. Because deep down, underneath it all, I'd been *hoping*. I had my roots dyed regularly, never wore long cardigans and didn't have a single cuddly animal on my bed. So I'd already taken the first, vital steps. Now it was really only a matter of time before I ceased resisting, gave way to the inevitable and let myself be happy.

★　★　★

I stayed at home for a few days, mulling things over. Eventually I psyched myself up and dialled his number. As I waited, I noticed the light on my answer-phone was flashing.

'Hello?'

'OK,' I said. 'Let's do it!'

'Did you get my message?'

'Not yet.'

'Ah. About the — job offer . . . '

'No . . . Congratulations.'

I stopped, felt my face tingle and my chest tighten.

'Where?'

'Bristol.'

13

Suspension Bridge

'It's not that far.'

'It's 120 miles.'

'It's just over an hour on the train.'

'Yeah but there's getting to Paddington as well . . . '

'You can come every weekend.'

'I may not always be free. I have a life here, you know. I can't just drop everything and rush off to Paddington every five minutes.'

'You don't have to drop anything. I'll get a really nice place, and make you a workspace.'

'With my own light? I need a proper light.'

'With a proper light.'

I went up to see him on his first weekend there, and we had a calm conversation about flats, and trains, and second word processors, and lovely views, and how I could work anywhere. And I agreed it would be fine. Then we got to Sunday and time to go to the station and I went into the bathroom and began crying and just couldn't stop.

I knew I couldn't do it: the endless goodbyes, getting off the train and getting used to each other again, then tearing myself away. I knew because I'd done it before.

I had commuted to stay with my father for several years from the age of five, leaving my mother and sister every Friday in a ritual so painful it became a permanent part of me. All this time I'd been looking for a catch with Peter, expecting something to go wrong. Now it had, it was almost a relief. He was going to move away and once again I was supposed to love someone and part from them, over and over again. Of course! That was always going to be my fate. I knew how we repeatedly bring about the things we most fear but secretly desire. But knowing had done me no good. When I met him, there was absolutely no sign that he would be offered a job elsewhere. He didn't work for a foreign company. He wasn't unreliable, secretly married, a serial seducer or a bolter. Yet somehow I had ended up in this situation again. And I deserved it. Separation was agony, and yet addictive. It was who I was.

I formed a plan. I'd go along with it for the moment, say nothing, and just gradually fall out of touch. I'd make sure I had something to do in London most weekends — I did anyway — until he got the message. There'd be no need for any emotional stuff. No one would have to be 'chucked'. He'd eventually

75

forget about me or meet someone else; with his new job to think about, he might not even notice. And I'd be spared the much bigger pain of losing him over and over again, or losing him later in some other way. This was better. This was good. I had control of it. I went back to London and got on with my life.

14

Capturing the Castle

I got away with it for a few months, then one Friday he rang and asked if I was coming up for the weekend.

'Oh, I can't. I've got a thing.'

'Again?'

There was an uncomfortable pause.

'What's going on?'

'Nothing — just, you know.'

'I thought we were going to move in together.'

Oops. I'd forgotten he had this thing about communicating. I only communicated for a living; I kept my private life nice and obscure.

I mumbled something about not liking goodbyes, and stations, and not having found the second word processor, and it probably being easier all round if we just let it go.

There was an awestruck silence.

'Is that what you want?'

He seemed to be a bit shocked.

'Well, not really. No. I just — '

'I thought you loved me.'

'Um, I do.'

I felt really silly now, as if I'd been caught drawing on the biology lab wall. Although we were on the phone and he couldn't see me, I looked down at my shoes.

'Well, for God's sake come up here and let's talk about it. And if you can't do that I'll come down there.'

Talk about it?

I didn't know how. As a girl in my therapy group had put it:

'For someone who talks such a lot you don't say much.'

When I got to Temple Meads he put his arms round me, kissed me, and steered me to the Citroën.

'We're going out to dinner. But first, we have a very important task to perform.'

I could tell by his tone of voice it was going to be something nice, but what?

'You want to get out of that flat, don't you? Well, now's your chance. Keep it on, so you don't feel you're burning your boats — it's dirt cheap, right? And bring some stuff up here. Clothes. Books. Women's things.'

We had a standing joke about my reluctance to unpack. He had been there four months and so far I had installed a toothbrush, a T-shirt and some tights.

'All right,' I said. 'Anyhow, we can't split up. I've still got your video recorder.'

I'd never had one before: it was amazing.

'You like the place here OK?'

He had rented a ground-floor flat with a dinky little kitchen and a huge double sitting room with more than enough space for an extra desk. It was near the shops and the Clifton Suspension Bridge. I loved it.

'And we can have lovely trips to Cheddar Gorge, and the woods, and the beach, and the cliffs at Clevedon. And there's that funny little cinema you like, and the Spanish wine bar. And I've found another good place for coffee . . . '

'You're right,' I said. 'You're right. It's going to be fine. I'm just a bit — you know.'

'I know. Me too. Meeting the person you want to spend the rest of your life with is a really big deal. But you're not doing it on your own, remember: we're doing it together. I'm here with you, all the way.'

The parachute was strapped on: I was as safe as I could be. If Brunel could span the Avon Gorge, surely I could manage this.

He drove to John Lewis, and guided me up to the bathroom department.

'What was that book you and your sister had such a thing about? About the two sisters?'

'*I Capture the Castle*?'

'Yeah.'

'And what is it they go on about, that represents grown-up, married life? That whatsername — '

'Rose, the heroine's sister.'

'Rose — wants.'

We had stopped in front of the towels.

'Towels! Matching towels!'

'Get a whole set. Go on: any colour.'

Rose and Cassandra's dream had been peach. I chose a beautiful, slatey blue. We went for dinner, then came back to the flat and arranged them in fat, luscious piles.

When I told my sister, she said:

'Staple him to the bed. He is definitely The One.'

The next key development happened not in John Lewis but Habitat. I agreed to marry him.

★   ★   ★

When I was eleven, the man my mother had just started living with dropped dead of a stroke. They weren't married. In fact, though very much separated, he hadn't got around to getting divorced, and his wife got the money and the house. The other house, the one we'd all been going to live in, went straight back on the market and we came back to London, to the flat which, luckily, we hadn't let go. My mother's lack of anger about her circumstances was characteristic; she didn't see them as something she could influence, and had never exerted pressure on him to sort things out.

But when I thought about that time now, I realized there were several very strong arguments in favour of going legal. I did a bit of research and discovered that one, there was no such thing as a 'common law' wife; however long you lived with someone, you still had no rights over their estate. If they paid the mortgage, it was their house, period. Two, if you bought a property with them and they died, their next of kin, who might well be their parents, could force you to move out and sell so they could inherit their half. And three, which really haunted me, if you died, the father of your children, if not married to you, did not automatically have the right to bring them up.

I digested this information and waited for a suitable moment to bring it up. I knew he was going to ask me again, so I could say yes without ruining the romantic atmosphere and bring the practical stuff up later.

We were looking for a rug. They were hung up on big horizontal wooden poles like the newspapers in a brasserie, and as he asked me, I lost my nerve a bit and hid amongst them. Eventually he pulled them aside and said, 'Oh go on! I promise not to ruin your independence.'

'Well,' I said. 'I've been looking into this and it does seem that however long you live with someone, you have no rights over their estate if they die. If you buy a property together and they die, their parents can force you to sell up so they can get their half. And if we had children and weren't married, and something happened to me, you wouldn't automatically be able to bring them up. Which is an awful thought.'

He looked at me, sandwiched between a striped cotton and a Berber twist.

'So that's a Yes, is it?'

I was glad it had happened while shopping; it made it feel more manageable, less momentous. And when I got back to London, instead of feeling bereft and faintly anxious, I felt wonderful. Could marriage actually make me feel more secure? Happier? Wow. What an amazing thought. Hey — maybe that explained why it was so popular. Ye-ah . . . the more I thought about it, the more sense it seemed to make. Wherever I was, we would still be together: joined. If I ever felt wobbly, I could just remember this and I'd be OK. This concept really had something going for it. It offered emotional security, financial stability

— and cake. Now I thought about it, I could really see why it had caught on.

We started telling people.

Friend 1: 'Oh my God ... that's wonderful!'

Friend 2: 'What?!'

Friend 3: 'You?! You're kidding ... '

Mother: 'Oh!' (overcome by emotion)

Nanny: 'Oh! Oh!!' (ditto)

Father: (before throwing his arms round Peter)

'Is this a joke?'

15

Incident at Wangaratta

Peter said:

'We have to tell Jason!'

Jason was his best friend. They'd known each other since school. He was a sculptor and he was funny. Peter was always quoting things he'd said, amusing, unusual things that made me feel, well, a bit jealous. If there was anyone in Peter's life I felt awed by, it was him. And because he'd married an Australian several years previously and gone back there with her, we'd never met.

'We'll go and see him!'

'Yeah, right. I know he lives in Australia.'

'No, I mean it. I've been meaning to go for ages. And now I've got the perfect excuse.'

'What, me?'

'Yes, you! The woman I'm going to marry.'

★ ★ ★

We met them in Sydney: Jason and his wife Victoria. They had a little boy, Vince, who was spending a few days with her sister. They drove us to Bondi, and then to Bronte, the smaller beach next door. We went to a café and drank long blacks and flat whites, and talked. The Staple Singers were on the music system, singing 'Come Go With Me'. All right! I thought: I will! Then we walked around in the bright sunshine and talked some more.

Then we went to a party at Victoria's cousin's house, and in the morning we got into the Volvo estate and drove to Melbourne.

But we never got there.

Well, we did, but the last bit of the journey was by ambulance.

It was three days before Christmas. The sun was shining. It had rained, briefly. We stopped to buy some fruit — cherries — and browsed around an old-fashioned general store. A friend back home had just had a baby and I bought her a handmade pram quilt with a swan on it. Even then I knew I was partly buying it for myself, to see what it felt like to hold something for a baby; now, anything seemed possible. It was all, like the road, stretched out before us.

When we got back into the car, Peter took over at the wheel. He and Jason had bought and sold cars together in the past, and trusted each other's driving absolutely. We ate the cherries as we drove along, not particularly fast, putting the stones into a paper bag between the seats. In the back were our bags and all the Christmas presents, from us to them, and them to us, and for their five-year-old, Vince.

Peter looked down to put a cherry stone in the bag.

The last thing I remember was the car veering suddenly to the left, on to the loose gravel that they used there in place of a hard shoulder. I learned afterwards that as we veered over, he over-corrected, skidding and sending us into a vertical somersault. Could something that heavy flip into the air? It could.

We ended up upside down, slammed against an emergency phone box. The picture made the front page of the local paper, *The Wangaratta Chronicle*. Luckily it wasn't in colour.

Everything was covered in glass, petrol and blood. By some fluke, none of us was killed, though we didn't know it at the time: Jason and Victoria couldn't see us, and vice versa, and we were all taken to different hospitals. I lost a lot of blood from my head and part of my scalp. Jason had a broken leg and was also bleeding from the head. Victoria had a broken sternum. Although he could hardly stand, Peter was breathalysed and spent one night in intensive care before being declared — physically at least — unscathed.

I woke up briefly in the ambulance, then again in the Royal Melbourne Hospital. My head hurt like hell. I had absolutely no idea what had happened. When Peter appeared at my bedside on the second day, I was still in a sort of dream — partly no doubt the morphine, but also a kind of suspended disbelief. A doctor told me I'd been in an accident, which seemed absurd. Peter showed me a picture of the car, which was all crumpled. If I couldn't remember it, how did I know it was true? I didn't even phone my parents to reassure them that I was alive.

There was evidence though: a clot somewhere near the brain but not, so far, affecting it. I'd been put on anti-convulsants. My head was shaved, and I had a bandage over the rectangular scar on my thigh where they'd taken some skin to graft on to my skull; even with the seatbelt, the top left portion of my scalp had been sheared off when we landed on the roof. Also, my head leaned way over to the right and wouldn't turn from side to side; to look at anything I had to turn my whole body. And a conjunctival haemmorhage had turned my left eye red, which along with the scratching and limping, lent the whole look a touch of badly acted pub menace.

Peter said:

'I'm really sorry.'

'That's OK.'

There weren't any mirrors on the ward, or I might not have forgiven him so quickly.

After I got out of hospital I was invited to recuperate at the house of Victoria's sister's friend Annie, my daily routine a bath, a tram ride to the physio, then back again. If I was feeling adventurous, Peter would take me out for coffee and cake. About six weeks after the accident, I had to take a taxi — something I dreaded — and I asked the driver to slow right down, because I was somewhat nervous in cars, having had a pretty serious bang on the head and almost broken my neck.

'Blimey,' he said. 'You suing the driver?'

'Actually, no,' I said. 'I'm marrying him.'

It always got a good reaction, that line.

The Australian doctors said I wouldn't be half-bald for ever. There was a treatment that could regrow the lost bit of my scalp, but it was slow and painful; I'd have to wait at least six months, till I was back in England, and stronger.

'I think,' I said to Peter, 'we're going to have to postpone the wedding.'

'I know you're scared of commitment,' said my therapist. 'But that was a bit drastic, even for you.'

We put it back a year, during which three

things happened: I discovered that being cared for by others was not weak and humiliating, but really, really nice. I'd been brought up never to sit down and let people wait on me, so hospital was a treat. And I didn't have to eat the food either: my sister Claire flew 12,000 miles to feed me ice cream and read me to sleep. Even the people whose job it was to care were amazing. I couldn't believe the nurses didn't want anything in return for all the lifting and injecting and wiping, and missed them when I left.

Meanwhile, Peter had the insurance company to deal with, the responsibility for having nearly killed the four of us, and the dreadful flashbacks. And once I was out, we both found that the role of carer was thankless and tedious. One day, making lunch, he succumbed to compassion fatigue.

'I suppose I'd better do your chicken then,' he sighed.

'*My* chicken?!' I yelled. 'Sorry if I'm a bother!'

He threw the chicken pieces at the wall and we watched the bloody juices drip down it. Then we laughed.

The second thing was that I couldn't manage on my own in London, so my move to Bristol became, for the time being, permanent.

'Some people are driven apart by events like this,' said Peter, 'whereas we've been brought closer together.'

'Only because I can't cross the road on my own,' I said.

The third thing was that at the end of that second winter, five months before the wedding, my father died of a heart attack.

'Well, that's that,' I said. 'We can't go ahead now.'

'Yes we can,' said Claire and Peter. 'We need something to look forward to.'

We went up the aisle together, me in a red dress and black veil — black net, £4.99 a metre, John Lewis — with a full head of hair. The soundtrack was Prokoviev's 'March of the Capulets', and the guests quietly snuffling. My sister read out a sonnet she'd written about our dad, and the atmosphere was so charged with emotion that when we came out into the sunshine it felt like a metaphor: out of the darkness and into the light. We were alive, and in love, and — in between the snuffling — full of joy as we began the rest of our lives together.

16

Scenes From a Marriage

Peter and I have a row, a really bad one. We've had lots of rows, but this one is so bad that somewhere in the middle of it I throw a plate into the fireplace, and threaten to leave him and take the children. It's like a storm blowing up on an apparently sunny day. How do we get from relative calm to full-blown, furious yelling?

Eventually he says what he always says.

'You've got to do something about your anger, you know that?'

And he grabs the car keys and goes out.

I go into the sitting room to watch TV. I feel horrendous. I need something to take my mind off the poison flowing through my veins. I need comedy.

I end up watching *Scenes From a Marriage* by Ingmar Bergman.

Actually, why not? It can't make me feel any worse.

As my sister once said when she arranged a smear test and a dental appointment on the same day:

'I'm going to feel horrible anyway; I might as well make a day of it.'

Ingmar Bergman was married five times and had numerous relationships while married.

'I have come to realize I have no talent for marriage,' he admitted in an interview, and you can just hear all the women in his life, chorusing — in Swedish of course:

'Well, der!'

Although he was a film director, *Scenes From a Marriage* was a six-part TV drama, made in 1973. I used to like his films — enjoy isn't really the right word — and I'm sure there are deep insights in these episodes from which I can learn. And even if there aren't, I shall just wallow.

The opening scene shows Marianne and Johan, a successful, articulate couple, being interviewed by a journalist for a magazine. The husband, who's evidently some kind of intellectual celebrity, is saying what a good husband and father he is. Urgh! Already he reminds me of Peter, whom I have decided never to speak to again.

'Do you ever argue?' asks the journalist and I can't believe what he replies:

'Marianne does.'

The exact same thing as Peter says to me! 'You're having this argument with yourself' is one of his favourite phrases, which explains why I want to kill him. It's not only infuriating in its own right, but chimes exactly with the thing my mother does of looking at me when I criticize her for some shortcoming during an argument and telling me, always in her most concerned voice,

'You appear to think people are against you.'

It's a brilliant technique for disempowering your opponent and winding them up to the point where they tremble with rage; try it sometime and you'll see what I mean. It's especially effective when delivered regretfully, with the head slowly shaken. Favoured by the Victorian patriarchy and dictatorships the world over for disabling and imprisoning dissidents, the 'You are mad' strategy has no equal.

In the next part of the drama, they're having dinner with another couple who are in the throes of splitting up; they go from apparently teasing each other to being really vicious, and the wife ends up throwing her brandy in her husband's face. Drunk and dishevelled, they eventually leave, and Johan and Marianne discuss their problems while doing the washing-up.

'It's their failure to communicate,' says Marianne.

And still we have no clue that anything is amiss in her own marriage — well, apart from the fact that her husband's a smug arsehole.

Then I realize I must have drifted off to sleep because suddenly Johan is leaving her for someone else. And she's begging him not to go, and it's awful. They've gone from perfect couple to disintegration — just like that.

While I rewind to find the point where it went wrong, it occurs to me what a horribly appropriate metaphor that is: falling asleep. I mean, that's what happens to quite a lot of us, isn't it? We get stuck in various routines, stop noticing or appreciating the other person and, worst of all, stop trying to be interesting, only to awake one day and find the cases being packed.

Peter and I say, 'Oh, it won't happen to us,' but that's what everyone says. It's what my parents said. We all want to believe we're immune to the deadly divorce virus, and if we just keep doing the same things each day, we'll get through. How many of us have thought of asking, 'Are things OK with us, *really*?' but decided against it, because we're afraid of what the answer might be? Better to keep your head down and hope for the best. But of course that's exactly the strategy that doesn't work. You have, as my friend Mark says, to take a good, long look under the bonnet — even though you're afraid of what you may find.

I rewind, go forward a bit. Ah, I've found it. Johan is going away to a conference but he's not going alone.

He says, 'I've gone and fallen in love.'

He looks slightly bewildered, as if it's the result not of banal, middle-aged lust but some outside force, like the weather. And for a few minutes you almost feel a bit of sympathy for him. He's been taken by surprise, he didn't mean it to happen, and so on. Marianne, clearly in shock, tries to organize his packing. And that's when he loses his temper, suddenly, as men sometimes do when women witter on about some horrendously unimportant detail. You want to shake her. Your husband's leaving you for a 23-year-old student, you stupid cow! Stop talking about jackets and thump him! That's where Bergman is so clever; he forces *you* to feel the emotion.

At some point she says how she can't believe she never noticed anything, and he says,

'You've never been particularly observant,' which is just *so* damning. He's got that same assumption of superiority as Peter; because he sounds 'rational', his viewpoint carries more weight. How many women have been told by their husbands, 'I can't talk to you when you're like this: you're too emotional'? When they're the cause of it! I'm stirred up, but feeling at least a bit better, since Bergman understands this dynamic. I wouldn't marry him, but he knows what makes men and women tick.

At this point Peter comes back from wherever he's been, sits down really heavily on the sofa, takes one look at Johan and says,

'Well, there's his problem; those pyjamas.'

He can't bear pyjamas. And I'm forced to agree with him, even though the way he says it, in the middle of this intense drama, is really irritating. He really does think it amusing to interrupt the middle of a really classy bit of cinema with this sort of facetious remark. And we had been having a row. You don't just come back in as if nothing's happened.

Of course, all the time you're watching this you're thinking: this smug git with a beard — who wears *brown* pyjamas — is leaving *Liv Ullman??*

'Liv Ullman!' I say. 'I mean, look at her.'

'Hmm,' he says. 'Not really my type.'

'Is that all you can say? You really are an idiot, you know that?'

Liv Ullman isn't just beautiful: she has that

celestial glow that only a few stars have, a sort of inner light. And it's a sort of proof of Johan's twattishness that he actually does leave her. As my friend Louise succinctly put it,

'If Bill ever left me, it would show that he wasn't the man I thought he was, and therefore I wouldn't ever want him back.'

I reflect on this and shudder.

Then Peter picks up the remote.

'Can we whizz forward and see if there's a fight?'

I grab it back.

'How about this?' I say. 'Can you just fuck off?'

I've spent twenty years trying to get him to appreciate films that don't have any explosions or car chases in them — never mind subtitles — and this is what he says. And clearly I'm supposed to give a tinkly laugh and say something like: 'How can I be angry with you? You're so incredibly amusing.' But I don't. He's already ruined my evening and now he's ruining this as well.

'Just get out of my sight, will you?'

What am I *doing* with this man?

He looks at me uncertainly and slopes off upstairs.

I watch the end of Johan and Marianne and sit staring at nothing for a while. I do love him but why are we arguing so much? And what happens if we can't stop? Will we end up as one of those couples who go through the motions, pretending to the children that things are fine, but biding our time, waiting for them to grow up so we can get as far away from each other as possible? I sit and think, but I don't know. We're stuck like this and I don't know how we're going to make it right. In the short term, it's eleven p.m. and I have to decide whether I'm going to sleep with him in our bed tonight or not. Last time we argued like this I stayed down here on the sofa and woke up with a really stiff neck. I hang around some more, then tiptoe upstairs. He's asleep and I slip in beside him. I may *appear* to have forgotten our differences, but I lie with my back to him so that when he does wake up, he won't think he's forgiven.

17

Make, Do and Mend

Peter believes we learn how to be married the same way we learn how to cook or fix cars: by example. And I agree. Looking at my parents, it would certainly explain a lot. Neither of them knew how to be married, or more important, how to stay married happily. My mother knew how to stay married, but only contemptuously.

After a good start, her parents grew apart completely. They didn't have anything in common or, she says, even like each other. According to her, they only coincided to sit silently opposite each other at the dinner table, then pursued totally separate interests: bridge and theatre in Granny's case, and golf in my grandfather's.

'On a good day,' as she once put it, 'they warmed up to indifference.'

I certainly never saw any affection expressed between them when I was a child, but then I'd never seen any between my own parents either. The first time I saw a married couple kiss each other I was shocked.

My dad's side was lacking in a more dramatic way. When he was very young, about six or seven, his father was taken away to a psychiatric hospital with something like Alzheimer's. Though still only in his fifties, he never returned home. Then the war came and Dad was evacuated, so separated from his remaining parent, and not happily. His mother was loving but pretty controlling and intense, and he had a similarly over-involved relationship with his sister who was emotionally disturbed. What the marriage was like before his father got ill no one can tell me now, but Dad seems to have grown up with little idea of how to compromise, or improve a relationship by modifying his behaviour. He and my mother had a great rapport, but once married, they set each other off. If only they hadn't married, they wouldn't have had to get divorced, and so could have had the friendship they eventually ended up having anyway.

When I met Peter, and experienced the little, day-to-day instances of kindness that underpin a successful partnership, I was bowled over. I hadn't been ill-treated by all his predecessors; I just hadn't come across consideration expressed as a conscious policy. All he had to do was come in and make me a cup of tea and I felt like a million dollars. And

I was staggered by the pay-off when I did something nice for him. You could improve the quality of a relationship simply by doing something for the other person, just like altering a recipe. So I wasn't getting the icing on the cake, but a totally different cake.

Why had no one told me this before? Actually, my mother had told me: I just didn't understand how it worked. And I didn't see it bringing about any change in my father or those who came after. If anything, she unwittingly demonstrated its downside: that being extra nice to men who aren't nice themselves doesn't make them behave better, but worse.

The private jokes and banter that brought my parents together wasn't an element in the world shared by Peter's parents. His mother wore an apron, his father smoked a pipe. They married at the start of the war, and he made almost all their furniture. The first time he described them, I thought, my God: they're the parents in the Ladybird books I learned to read with, the ones with titles like *Things We Like* and *Look at This*. My parents may have been funnier, but his set a better example. They didn't yell at each other: they had hobbies. My parents didn't have hobbies unless you count screaming. Perhaps an occasional game of tennis, or the odd jigsaw puzzle, and they might not have needed to fall in love with other people. And yes, I do I realize I sound like a pre-war information film on the prevention of masturbation:

'*Keeping young minds — and bodies — busy is the key to maintaining a clean and healthy life.*'

To get the full picture of these people, who shaped him into the husband he is today, I ask him:

'What do you remember them doing when you came home from school?'

'Well, I don't remember them having conversations all the time the way we do.'

'Not *talking*? What were they doing?'

'My mother was always sewing. My father was *always* in the garage making something. Or developing his photos in the bathroom. Or mending something. A great deal of their time was taken up with mending. I remember him bursting into my room one morning and saying, ''I've mended my pacamac for two and six!''

'Good grief.'

'They were kept occupied by the constant need to keep things going. I remember him cleaning a blocked tea strainer with a pin. It was only a plastic one, but he was so satisfied at having restored it.'

'Ooh,' I say. 'Another exciting evening in.'

'You did ask.'

'God! So defensive!'

'They had zones of expertise and control, which were very clearly defined. My father never cooked anything until after she died.'

He thinks this is one reason why they hardly ever had a row.

'The opportunities for conflict are far greater now,' he says, 'because the boundaries are blurred.'

'So,' I say. 'Do you think that nowadays, now that people have far more time on their hands and don't have to unblock their tea strainers with pins, they have to find things they have in common, things to do together, to avoid getting bored? Maybe it's another reason marriages appear to be under more strain.'

He gives me a wary look, as if I'm about to get us into trouble.

'I'd be really careful about generalizing if I were you.'

'All *right*! It's only a theory. God . . . '

I hate it when he goes all pompous like that. I just agreed with him! Anyhow, what's going to happen if I generalize for two seconds? The Generalizing Police are going to burst through the door and take me away? I'm only making the same point he was, about his parents having separate interests. Mine expected more from each other, in some ways, and didn't make it.

Ultimately, all I'm saying is, those men you see at weekends, trailing round M & S or Homebase behind their wives, or just standing silently outside changing rooms like Antony Gormley sculptures, forty years ago would have been in their garages making shelves. Or at least tinkering with something. It's a fairly recent development that men and women — in any numbers at least — are thrown together so much. And so maybe our expectations have changed and maybe there's more room for disappointment.

Anyhow, I only said *maybe*.

18

Boeuf Bourguignon with Herbie Hancock (*Lucy and Jon*)

Twenty years ago, if you'd told me I was going to end up married to a half-Welsh Yorkshireman with an extensive collection of model cars, I would have said even *I* could do better than *that*.

And yet, two decades later, here we still are.

So much for 'compatibility'.

Based on compatibility, I should be with Jon. My friend Lucy lives with Jon. He's very intelligent, likes jazz and jazz fusion, has a hairy chest — ish — and cooks like a pro. To experience his *boeuf bourguignon* is to enter a higher dimension of ecstasy. But does Lucy appreciate him? She doesn't even like red meat. When I come round, and he puts on a CD he knows I'll like, she rolls her eyes and hurls herself into her seat. But they are happy together, more or less, and so — most of the time — are we.

I am, of course, simplifying this hugely; just because Jon can do not only classic French food but also proper curries, and likes early-to-middle period Herbie Hancock, doesn't mean I could fall in love with him. And it would be misleading to say he and Lucy have little in common. They both love, for example, camping, which I would only ever do if our house was destroyed by a freak blending accident. And they share a laid-back, hippyish attitude to life, which would eventually — or really quite quickly — drive me mad.

'You would have *hated* it,' she says with relish, whenever they come back from one of their holidays in some kaftan-wearing, tented community.

But we all know this and laugh about it, so that's OK.

I am asking her to tell me what *doesn't* work in their relationship, because I want to make a comparison. And also I want to confirm my suspicion that Peter, the husband people keep telling me I'm so lucky to have, is not after all this Superspouse. I bet that most of the shortcomings of Jon, or any other man, are no worse than his. He just spins better.

We're in her kitchen, where I first sat and ate her homemade flapjacks after we'd just met. We had only recently moved across the Thames to this area where I knew no one. Lawrence and Lucy's son Milo were then two, his little sister Lola was not yet born, and Lydia was only one. And I was still feeling weary, homesick and alone. Then outside Treetops Nursery I realized I had found someone very special: funny, intelligent, perceptive, and refreshingly honest. Plus she offered me a beer at five p.m. Since having children, I had discovered that mothers could be divided very clearly into two on this, between those who would offer you a drink after school and those who wouldn't give you a brandy if you were buried in the snow. We bonded immediately over that, but didn't get on to the failings of the men in our lives for some time; the children were still small and it took all our energy to work through the numerous problems we had with them.

She and Jon have been together since just before Milo was born. They met in India, where she was originally meant to be teaming up with someone else. That's another difference between us: I could never say to someone, 'See you in India.' The first time I went to meet Peter in Sheffield I was consumed by anxiety because I thought 160 miles was too far from London for him to remember me.

They met in India, but only for a day the first time, because they both had to go their separate ways. But they realized they were smitten and, having got back to England, arranged to return to that extraordinary country, and to meet up again. How romantic!

She complains about him a fair bit, and they snipe at each other a little, but it's nothing compared with me and Peter. They have, I would say, an above-average relationship.

'So, seeing as I think Jon has a lot going for him,' I say, 'what don't you like?'

'When we're about to go out,' she says, 'and we're literally on the doorstep, he goes on to Multimap to find the way. We then have to wait fifteen minutes for our incredibly slow printer, and so are always late.'

'Hmm,' I say. 'That's quite annoying.' Though not, I think, as annoying as Peter's delusion of believing every journey takes twenty minutes. And not as annoying as my habit of thinking I can rely on my memory, which used to be amazing but is now rubbish, and running out the door having glanced briefly at an address, setting off with a vague idea of where we're going and then realizing that I don't actually know where it is.

Her next complaint I cannot go along with. 'He comes in and says, 'So what needs doing round the house, then?' Can't he *look*?'

My God: she lives with a man who even *asks*? I know I am lucky — I admit it — but some husbands we know still don't lift a finger. Forty years after they were divorced — and fifteen years after his death — my mother still mentions the fact that my father never cleaned the loo. And let's face it, none of them do. If you're reading this and you are a man who does — not counting if you live on your own — or you're married to a man who does, then e-mail me. I'll send you a free bottle of Toilet Fuck. I mean Toilet Duck. Can you believe I typed that without even realizing?

'When I'm doing housework, like cleaning the floor, he comes up behind me and sticks his hand between my legs.'

'Well, that's your fault for cleaning the floor.'

You can just tell I've been married for *ages*, can't you? A newly-wed would ask why he doesn't do it more. The only time I'm ever to be found in the provocative, bending position is when I'm reading the papers Peter's just put in the recycling box.

Her next complaint is perhaps the one I've heard from women more than any other.

'He's good with the kids now, but when they were younger he did absolutely nothing.

I used to have to threaten to leave him just to get him to take them to the park.'

I remember a woman at school once telling a group of us she was getting a divorce. Top of her list of his failings was that her husband worked all week, then at weekends vanished off to see the football. When I talked to him, he claimed he spent every weekend in close attendance, including putting them to bed. Which version was true? I never found out. At least in Jon's case you can see he adores his kids.

'And,' I say, 'he can cook.'

That's my answer to everything. A man can be a politician or have the physique of a rhinoceros, but if he can do *boeuf bourguignon*, I'll be his slave. Jon can do *boeuf bourguignon*, and *coq au vin*, and —

'Yeah,' she says, 'but he's got a really limited repertoire.'

Good God, woman, he can do a proper curry! Thai *and* Indian. Whenever I go round there, we talk about recipes. Well, not just recipes; he can talk about lots of things — food, books, music — everything, pretty much.

'Yeah, but he never bothers to read articles about anything we need to know about, like parenting. I have to do it.'

Well, show me a man who does. Peter never

reads that stuff either, and even says, 'Why don't you read it and tell me what it says?' as if his time is so much more valuable, whereas I'm expected to read news stories about the motor industry. It makes me want to roll them up and thwack him.

Also, Jon is quite intuitive. He takes an equal interest in the personal lives of their friends, rather than dismissing that territory as so many do. A lot of them have no radar for that at all. They can spend a whole evening with someone and not find out he's recently got divorced.

'When I have an emotional problem, he says, 'Deal with it.''

Mind you, Perfect Peter with his so-called emotional intelligence is hardly always ever Mr Supportive in practice. The minute I get remotely het up he goes all sort of uptight and official, as if our emotional output is being monitored by Ofsted.

'By the way,' I say, 'we've been at it for at least an hour and most of the things you don't like are, if I may say so, not very major.'

'Whenever I'm watching a film or something, he comes in and says, 'So what's this pile of shit?''

OK: no one likes having their taste disparaged.

'Oh yeah, he never buys me a birthday present.'

Men and presents are another minefield, full of pain and foreboding. Every year for the past few years, Peter has said very sincerely:

'Now, what do you *really want*?'

And I have replied, equally sincerely:

'I would really *love* a little trip somewhere.'

And he always looks slightly crestfallen, as if hoping that I might have changed my mind from the last time he asked me and now want something less ambitious, like a box of hankies or a smile.

'Or a night out,' I say. 'Even just a meal out, organized by you. You know, that I don't have to book.'

The crestfallen look then changes to one of blankness.

'A *surprise*,' I add, in case it's not crystally, abundantly clear.

And he has never done it. Not once. I'm not even thinking of Paris or Venice — or even the West End. There's a restaurant I really love a mile down the road in Clapham, for God's sake.

Yet, with finances tight and the children to think of, I can identify with her entirely when she says:

'But then I don't want him to get me a present, because it's our money . . .'

Exactly. You know there are other things you need far more. Priorities change, the point where you kept your money separate has long passed, and what once seemed romantic and thrilling now feels impractical and foolish. You have the feeling that if he did burst in the door brandishing the keys to a pink helicopter, you'd just sigh and remind him that the children need new coats. I think a lot of us feel that way. Having said that, we also do, now and then, like a *treat*. I'll never forget Peter, arriving home on one of the — by then — seventeen anniversaries when he hadn't brought me flowers, saying:

'I much prefer to do these things spontaneously, rather than on a specific day.'

Well, any time, mate, any time.

At this point I glance at my watch and realize it's time for me to take the children home. I don't want to go; Lucy understands me. When I'm with her I feel intelligent and perceptive, instead of inefficient and tired. And there's a vital question I need to ask.

In her most frustrated moments, would she ever consider shagging someone else?

'I couldn't,' she says immediately.

'Very commendable,' I say. 'Well done.'

'It'd mean a new man seeing my stomach.'

'Oh, right. Well, me too.'

I have long thought that fear of the

113

flab-on-view is the most effective adultery deterrent known to woman. Unfortunately it seems unlikely to work for men. I mean, can you imagine a man saying,

'I would have a shag on the side but for some woman seeing my beer gut'?

Let alone a small willy or any of the things men *are* traditionally supposed to dread.

'I could possibly consider it, though,' she says, 'if I found a man with a hugely obese wife.'

'Ah yes: you'd be sylphlike by comparison,' I say, though I should point out that she is actually a size twelve at most.

'You'll get no sympathy from me,' is my response when she moans about not being able to wear this or that garment before appearing the following day in a wrap-around dress. I've bought three wrap-around dresses and can't leave the house in any of them. The other difference is that whereas on her they look smart and sexy, on me they look like multicoloured cling film. Plus she's six years younger than me.

'Hmm,' I say, as I close my notebook. 'I'm afraid I have to conclude that he does suit you, and really isn't that bad.'

'Yeah, you're probably right,' she says. 'He is well informed, has opinions on everything, and does still laugh at my jokes.'

And surely that's what matters. I have been round there a hundred times and have never heard either of them sound bored. Well, apart from when Herbie Hancock is on, but as I say, sometimes it's better if you're not too compatible.

19

Flee Like This

Lydia's doing Water Skills 3 in swimming this week. Me, I'm still on Marital Skills 1: learning not to growl when Peter makes toast and leaves the bread out. I know it's not a big crime. As with the damp flannel he always leaves on the edge of the basin after shaving which goes smelly, it's a daily irritant; heart disease can kill you, but a bum itch will drive you mad.

As Lawrence would say, 'That's your fault for marrying him.'

It's all cause and effect with him, which is what comes of paying too much attention in Physics.

But when I think about the conversations I have with other, sometimes younger, people about not just boyfriends but also flatmates, it's clear that marriage is not solely to blame. There's something about the sheer condition of living with others — any others — that causes stress. Those who work with animals often say how much easier and more straight-forward they are than people — though quite often that's because they just hate people.

I think it's partly because we all like to be in control — and that includes those who appear not to be the controlling type. Take my old schoolfriend from way back, who once came to stay and was, on the face of it, adorable and full of common sense. The minute her suitcase was over the mat, she changed into a manipulative, passive-aggressive weirdo who would not communicate in a straightforward way. I know what you're thinking: first I say my husband has turned into my mother, and now I'm saying everybody else has, too.

What I do think is that proximity brings out the worst in — well, many of us, and it doesn't require the crucible of marriage. All you have to do is share a flat with a friend for a month, or go on holiday with another family, and the same conflicts arise. In the case of our house guest, she crept around, almost in a crouching position, as if expecting us to tell her off — why, I don't know — and begged humbly to be allowed to have a bath/make tea/grill a small triangle of toast, etc. until we did indeed eventually find her completely exasperating. By the time she left we could hardly bear the tap of her meek little feet. And she, no doubt, would say that we were rude, horrible hosts. But had she not come to stay, we would never have seen that side of her at all.

It's very clever of them, of course, because those who tiptoe through life never have to take the blame for anything. Just like the friend of my mother's who once drove us across a busy junction without looking, narrowly missing a police van and causing us all to go white with fear — they create chaos and fury around them. They don't crash; everyone else does. So when the PC pulled her over — with some difficulty as she still wasn't looking — she said sweetly, 'Gosh, officer, do you mean me?'

All right, I'm not saying Peter's *that* bad. I admit I'm bossy and controlling. I admit that I tell people how to do things when they don't need me to. I admit everything, OK? I just do wish he would wrap up the bread when he's finished.

And he points out — no more often than is strictly necessary, of course — the rather more significant fact is that he actually *makes* toast in the first place, and not just toast but bacon sandwiches/scrambled eggs/sausages for me and the kids every morning. Therefore I Should Be Grateful and stop whingeing about the unwrapped bread. And I know, not that I ever tell him this, that he is right.

But how many couples, after more than ten

years together, manage never to dwell on the negative? Am I the only one who's come into the house when he's had the kids all day, and said:

'You've not tidied up, then.'

When they were small, Peter would say:

'I've got the children dressed!'

And I'd say:

'You've put Lydia in a dirty top.'

Well, come on, though: he could *look*.

I know men find it particularly irritating that women demand that they perform some task or other, then stand over them, telling them how to do it. It's got to the point where, when Peter's making breakfast — which he does every day: did I mention that? — if I so much as *look* at the cooker, he barks at me, as I do have a tendency to sneak up and turn down the gas. Sometimes I even lie in wait until he's on the other side of the room, getting a plate.

'It doesn't boil faster if you turn it right up,' I say. 'It's still 100 degrees.'

'JUST GET OVER THERE.'

'I would do more,' is the plea of several men I've met, 'if only my wife would just back off and let me!'

And we do let them, of course; we just like to help them along with a few pointers:

'Jamie only eats raw carrots, not cooked.

How can you not know that?'

Or:

'That's way too much butter!'

And my own, personal favourite:

'Why d'you always put the eggs and bacon in separate pans?'

It's not just kitchen things either. His handwriting is pretty awful, and last Christmas he was doing his cards — most men don't even bother, yes I know — and the addresses were barely legible. These'll never get there, I thought, so I completed some of the letters.

'Don't stand over me,' he said.

I also went through the stamped pile and added some of the surnames. And he said,

'What are you doing? Just leave them alone.'

'But you haven't put on their surnames.'

'Just leave me alone, will you?!'

And I can't even tell you what it was like the year he went self-employed. The deadline for filing your tax return got closer and closer, and still there was no sign of any activity. All over the country, people were bent over their office floors for the annual gathering of the receipts, and he hadn't even put his out. Eventually I said,

'Um, have you done your tax return?'

And he said,

'I'll get on to it.'

Two weeks later I asked him:

'Any progress on the tax return?'

'I'm on the case.'

A phrase I find particularly irritating in its refusal to reveal its true meaning: 'I have done nothing at all.'

'I'm only saying, because, you know, if it's late they fine you.'

I've been self-employed since I was eighteen, and have never been late.

'I'll get on to it, *OK*??'

'It's £100.'

And it's my money too.

'I tell you what, why don't I do it after I've DONE ALL THIS OTHER STUFF?'

'What other stuff?'

'I unblocked the drain, remember? Lay on the ground in the rain with my hand down it, scooping out the mud?'

'What, when you used my soup ladle? That was ages ago. Hang on, that wasn't even this house.'

And he says I don't finish things.

The things he says I *do* finish, which I *shouldn't*, are his stories. But I don't. I just sometimes make encouraging noises, say something like, 'This is really funny,' or fill in the bits he's left out, like the main point.

OK, I do come from a long line of women,

Jewish on one side and non-Jewish on the other, who would stand over their men telling them what to do. In the back of my mind I can hear their ancestral voices, one lot bossing their men west of the Urals — 'Why are you fleeing like that? Flee like this' — and the others, like my Scottish granny, addressing their menfolk in tones that would startle a sergeant major. I can still hear her, summoning my grandfather to tea, snapping out his name — '*Ian!*' — as if commanding a firing squad.

My mother's not bossy at all, in either a Jewish or non-Jewish way. But she is the Queen of Micro-management, her style being to wear you down with persistent, undermining questions, like land erosion. Peter put up a blind in her kitchen, and she stood about two inches behind him, giving instructions. She was so close that it looked like that scene in *Bringing Up Baby* where Cary Grant accidentally rips half of Katharine Hepburn's dress off and has to shadow her all the way out of the restaurant so no one can see her pants. Except in the movie it was funny. How is it that someone with no knowledge of a job can stand there and tell you how to do it? But that's never held her back. Whatever you're doing, she knows how to do it better. She could have stood over Brunel and told him how to build the Clifton Suspension Bridge.

'It looks awfully short. Are you sure it's going to reach all the way across?'

'Madam, it is as yet incomplete.'

We in my family are terrible at Letting Men Get On With Things. Not only do we not let them Get On With Things, when we *do* let them do something, we focus on what they've left out:

'Lovely bridge, Isambard, but look: you've missed out a tiny bit of paint just there.'

It's particularly ironic, when you think that all the parenting books recommend Positive Reinforcement, i.e., praising good behaviour rather than criticizing bad. And some of us have even tried it and found it works. It's just that couples tend not to use it on each other.

'Good, darling: you've managed to get through an entire parents' evening without picking your nose.'

Or:

'Well done: you stroked me for a three full minutes before demanding sex.'

Actually, most of the advice on sex I've seen really does say that. You mustn't say:

'You're rubbing me like someone using paint remover; I've lost all feeling below the waist.'

But:

'I love that gentle foreplay. Your finger work

is really coming along well.'

Or was that my piano teacher?

Besides, nagging is easier.

I remember seeing a TV programme years ago, way before *Wife Swap* and all those, about couples whose marriages were on the rocks. They submitted themselves to be filmed and to watch themselves afterwards with a counsellor, a radical idea then. In the one I saw, the man — or woman: they both did it — would come into the kitchen and make themselves a cup of tea; they'd never offer one to their other half. The counsellor pointed this out and it seemed sad, but also, in a way, quite heartening, that such a small thing could make a difference.

There was no follow-up, so I don't know if they started communicating better or ended up screaming all the way to the divorce courts. But it was sound advice. No matter how much we've snapped at each other I always make dinner and Peter always makes me a cup of tea in the morning — and, as I said earlier, breakfast, because with low blood sugar I can get a bit edgy. Like the islanders in *King Kong*, he knows to throw something edible over the wall at fairly regular intervals if he wants to make it to old age.

And I'm learning how to come up with suitable answers for all those times when he tries to make me responsible for some neutral irritant totally uncaused by me, such as when the children came back from the park with some small bits of tree they'd been playing with. And he said:

'By the way, have you got any plans for this collection of sticks?'

It really annoyed me, the way he made it seem as though he's the only one with a proper function in the house and I just take up space. So the only way to achieve parity in that instance would be to say,

'Yes: I'm using them to build pianos for musically gifted blind children.'

20

Can We Go Now?
(*Rachel and Steve*)

I met Rachel when she had her daughter Lottie at the same time as I had Lawrence. I was quite lonely and overwhelmed, and frequently on the verge of panic, so was impressed that she had somehow managed to keep her sense of humour. The sardonic way she referred to Lottie, as if she was an unpredictable new flatmate as opposed to a baby, was very entertaining. She had the ability to turn quite mundane irritations into a source of amusement. For example, her last job had been for a control freak who would stand over her while she made the tea. I knew she didn't really tick off 'put tea bag in water' on a clipboard, but Rachel's impression of her doing it was so funny it didn't matter.

The thing I noticed about her marriage, that I recognized from my own, was the Double Standard: the 'say one thing, do another', or the 'one rule for me, another for you' scenario. In Peter's case, though, I just call it part of the Big Fat Story he tells about himself, i.e. lies.

126

'When we go to a party,' she says, 'I hate the way Steve'll come up to me quietly and say 'Shall we go?' And then when I go round saying my goodbyes, he rolls his eyes at people and looks at me as though I'm the lightweight that can't keep up the pace and has to be tucked up in bed with a cocoa. I fall for it every time.'

That is quite annoying. Peter does the equally annoying opposite of that, which is to say, 'Now don't forget to signal me when you've had enough', or 'I'm pretty tired so let's not stay late.' Then, when I say, at a reasonable time, 'Well, I think we should go', he reacts as if he doesn't know what I'm talking about — even if he's actually dropping off at the table.

I'm not exaggerating here, by the way; he has fallen asleep at every kind of evening: party, dinner party, New Year's Eve party — you'd think the noise would have kept him awake — too many films to mention, and nearly every play we've ever seen. But more annoying than that is this studious ignoring of my waggling eyebrows and other signals, following *his* request not to leave too late in the first place. The only thing he hasn't done is say, 'Why are you kicking me under the table?' which a friend of my sister always did.

'If he's ever off work and at home with me,'

Rachel goes on, 'as soon as I have a cup of tea or sit down he'll say, 'If you're not busy, you can help me with repointing that brickwork' or 'If you're bored, you can come out and help me reorganize the shed.''

'Ah yes, the male assumption that the female never has anything important to do. Um, I do sometimes do that to Peter. If I'm going away — even just for the day — I get this sort of panic and start giving him things to do.'

'Oh dear,' she says.

I think I've just gone down in her estimation.

But I'm not the only one: a couple we met through school came round once and the bloke complained to Peter that at weekends his wife kept giving him lists of tasks. Peter took him aside, kindly, as if he was the new boy, and said,

'You don't want to be letting her do that.'

And the bloke looked at him blankly, and Peter said,

'Just ignore it!'

And he was really surprised, as if he didn't know you could, which is quite strange when you think how many marriages go through their whole length, possibly even to the grave, with a whole series of jobs still not done. I predict that when I eventually snuff it, the spare tiles to replace the missing ones in the hall floor will still be under the stairs with the tub of dried-up, shrunken grout, next to the pink CD player he got for Lydia on eBay that never worked.

Spending: now here's a contentious area.

'If I buy anything expensive,' Rachel says, 'I generally keep it to myself, so as not to be treated like Nick Leeson on the day he brought down Barings. But if *he* buys anything expensive he spends quite a long time lecturing me with the aid of flow charts on why, in the long run, we will all be better off and will thank him for his ingenuity and speculation skills.'

'Hah. Double Standard — I told you. That is *so* male!'

This is where I have to admit that Peter has never, ever told me off for spending money — not that I think I should be grateful. But I did know a woman who regularly lied about what things cost, including things for the family, like meat. She'd buy £25 worth of fillet steak and tell him it cost ten. They weren't poor, either. He'd come back from business trips with huge boxes of body cream and Chanel perfume. I saw them in the bedroom once, piled up like in a duty-free shop. Another friend of mine used to complain that whereas they could 'never afford' any treats or luxuries she wanted to buy, *he* would always get himself two or three CDs every Friday as if they were essentials the whole family had to have. This is what comes of women in the home not being valued.

Whoops! Here again, I find myself guilty of the husband's crime:

'When I go into any room after he's been in there it's like that scene in *Sixth Sense* where the mother comes back into the kitchen and all the doors and all the drawers have been left open. He is incapable of shutting a drawer or door.'

'Oh no! I get told off for exactly the same thing. Peter goes round spotting drawers that have been left sticking out two millimetres and tutting while closing them, as if he's some sort of Kitchen Standards Inspector.'

And it's often the children's fault, but I get blamed as if I'm another twelve-year-old. He has this way of somehow always casting himself in a morally superior role.

Rachel says Steve does that with the TV she watches, just as Lucy says about Jon. Is there a gene in the male chromosome that has to disparage women's choice of television?

'If there is any programme or film about World War I or II — about literally anything from the Enigma code to a portrait of Churchill's parrot — he will be watching,' she says.

'Don't talk to me,' I say. 'I've had twenty years of it.'

'And when I protest, to say could we have a change for once, he says, 'I can't understand how you can't be interested in the world around you,' as if I'm someone who finds the DNA tests on *The Jeremy Kyle Show* too challenging.'

'Ah. Well, that's not fair. And again, I have to admit Peter doesn't do that, though I am noticing an unspoken contest to see who can get more of their programmes on to the hard disk, which I am winning by encouraging the children to put on multiple episodes of things they and I like, such as *My Name is Earl*.'

Then when Peter comes in and finds twenty stored episodes of the top white-trash comedy, he calls through to the kitchen, in a plaintive tone:

'Any chance I could record something?' which is designed to garner sympathy but obviously has the opposite effect. Even the kids aren't taken in by that.

'On the rare occasions that I get to the TV first,' says Rachel, 'he will inevitably sigh and say, 'And this is what you want to watch, is it?' as though he's Richard Dawkins and I'm the Archbishop of Canterbury: 'withering' is the word.'

Peter doesn't try to wither me in that way, but he does something just as bad. Always in a conversation with other people rather than just us, he'll wait till I've finished, often looking away, then ask the other person something on a completely different tack, as if to prove that my contribution was pointless and irrelevant. For example, say I've just responded to someone else's point about reading schemes, or swine flu or bankers' bonuses. He'll leave a two-second gap, as if to clear the hard drive, and say to them:

'So! You going away this summer?' making me feel that my comment wasn't even worth a response, and switching the conversational points so it all heads off in another direction and no one else will respond to it either.

Perhaps Peter's special quality is the ability to be annoying in really original ways. Unusually for his sex, he doesn't mind shopping. He will even nip out and get that last-minute pot of cream I've forgotten, to put on a cake.

'If Steve and I are out shopping I need to pass food to him about every two hours or he is liable to get upset.'

Shopping has this effect on a lot of people. 'Peter will only go into certain shops. For some reason, he avoids Marks and Spencer. I've always assumed it's because the men's stuff is upstairs, but he claims it's that it's 'middle-aged' — which is not true of the underwear, as we all know.'

Mind you, *I* object to the larger branches, as they refuse to reveal the whereabouts of, say, suits, by the radical measure of having overhead signs that say: 'Suits'. Instead you have to find them by doing the equivalent of Indiana Jones with the Staff of Ra.

Second to shopping in the Marital Conflict ratings is queuing.

'He will never, *ever* stand in a queue. Trips to IKEA are out, as are ice creams for the kids. He has a tolerance threshold of about twenty seconds before he says,

'This is ridiculous: I'm not standing here!''

'I hate it too: I always feel I'm going to be trapped there for ever. Peter's the same, or rather, he will queue but becomes really pompous. Every time we've ever got on a plane, it starts with him joining the checkout queue and saying to me, all martyrishly,

'Why don't you go and get yourself a coffee?' as if I'm so selfish I'm incapable of sacrificing half an hour of my sacred time.'

Rachel's final story is, I imagine, *not* typical, but worth sharing just for the gasp factor:

'He did forget my name after I'd been going out with him for about three years. He went to an estate agent's to try to find us a flat to rent. And when the agent asked for his details he gave them, but couldn't remember mine. The agent said, 'And your girlfriend's name?' and he said he went blank. This made the estate agent look at him, which made him even more blank, which made the rest of the agents in the room stare at him, which made him even *more* blank. Finally, after several minutes, he eventually burst out with my name.'

'When he recounted this story to me later that day he said, 'The thing was, I could see your face: I just couldn't think of the name.''

'Does it say something for him?' I ask, 'that he told you?'

And we agree that it doesn't.

Actually, it took me about three years to remember that Peter took sugar in his tea — and then to unremember it again because he gave up — and I still sometimes forget the colour of his eyes.

I've just gone and checked: they're blue.

21

Animal Husbandry

One evening I was coming home from seeing a friend in town and I missed the last rush-hour train before they drop from five an hour to two, and after half an hour's wait at London Bridge I found my train had been cancelled, and so I got one to the next nearest stop on a line that was actually running, which is too far from the house to walk. I would have rung Peter to force him to fetch me from the station, but he was out. And as I waited at the bus stop, watching bus after bus go past because it was full, I reflected furiously how stupid I was ever to marry someone who would end up forcing me to live in a place with no tube station. If only I'd stayed in central London, I said to myself. I was lonely and there was a hole in the wall where the snow came in, but at least I could get there.

There are many, many things we don't consider before embarking on a long-term relationship, so many, in fact, that it would be pointless to try to list them here. And when you have children you have to multiply that number by infinity since the number of things children will disagree about, and that they will get *you* to disagree about as a result, is unlimited. Yet you blithely carry on making your wedding plans and arranging your place cards with absolutely *no idea what's coming.*

You think you've got it covered. You go:

'Well, we've discussed having children, and whether we'd ever want to live in the country, so . . . '

And when you first meet, you think:

'We both like shabby chic and Matt Damon films, so *that*'s OK.'

It's that compatibility again. A more useless concept was never invented.

And underneath the certainty, behind the thoughtless assumption that nothing is ever going to come up that you can't resolve, the issues are building. Like mines hidden in the garden, they bide their time, until CRASH! He decides you should start going to church to get them into a better school. Or BOOM! She thinks you should have five children instead of two. And BANG! His mother's going to come and live with you.

In my case, it's that twenty years ago I had lunch with a guy. And now I have pets.

Why do I have pets, you ask? When I am not a Pet Person.

I will tell you.

I have pets because of the evil alliance between my husband and the children, all part of his plan to line them up on his side and turn them against me. There I've been, worrying about consumerism, Facebook and hormones, when a far more insidious influence has been inside the family, inflicting its damage all along.

When I first met him, Peter had cats. Aha, you say, you should have known! But they were part of his previous life. When he moved to Bristol, they went to live with a nice lady called Jill. Incidentally, he can't have been that attached to them as he never even gave them names.

One evening, his sister Jessica came round to babysit and as we were leaving for the cinema, I overheard Lydia say:

'If Daddy and Mummy both die, will you and Joe look after us?'

'I should think so, yes,' said Jessica.

'Hooray!' said Lydia. 'Than we can have parents with pets.'

Joe and Jessica had a cat. She had had two cats and a dog in her previous marriage but as they died off, he had skilfully worked down the total. Now, there was a man I could live with.

So back when Peter's kittens were just two

fluffy memories, how could I possibly have anticipated that we'd end up with children and live animals? And that a certain child's desire to *have* live animals in the house was, thanks to her father, going to override my desire *not* to? To give you an arbitrary example, totally at random, from just the other day, at what point when you discover your husband has promised your daughter an *alpaca* for her fifteenth birthday would you feel the marriage was liable to come under strain?

(a) Really quite soon;
(b) Like, now;
(c) You promised her *what??!*

And yes, we do live in London.
And yes, Lydia is still only eleven.
But she has a very, very long memory.
And though it came up from time to time, I succeeded in keeping the whole idea on the hypothetical back burner until a couple of years ago when my mother — with no previous form in this area — suddenly bought Lawrence some phasmids. They looked like scorpions, but were a kind of stick insect, and lived on eucalyptus but also brambles, which was good because we had a lot of those.
OK, it wasn't Peter. My mistake was not to

138

protest. I should have rung her up and said, 'He's nine: he doesn't need an entourage.'

I didn't make any noises whatsoever, until they started suddenly dropping dead on their perches. Branches. Whatever.

From the moment of their arrival on Lawrence's birthday, they were the centre of attention. Despite not being a Pet Person, and therefore supposedly unsympathetic to their lot, I actually hate seeing any creature in a box or cage, and feel pity for their lack of freedom, but also slightly feared these ones, because of their creepy and sinister appearance. But I kept this to myself and simply avoided that part of the house, which was slightly tricky as they were right by the door to the loo.

But everyone else liked them. And there was a certain cachet to be had from owning pets who were so unusual, yet also incredibly low maintenance and easy to feed. The children's friends who came for play dates were always fascinated and impressed.

However, one day while at the school gate waiting for Lawrence, I got a call from Peter. He was at home and sounded awful.

'What's happened?' I said. 'Are you all right?'

'Have you got Lawrence yet? Don't say anything to him,' he said, 'but I think one of the phasmids is dead.'

'Oh no! How?'

'I don't know. I feel *terrible*,' he said, his voice catching.

When we got back, he was red-eyed. Lawrence went straight to the glass tank as he did every day after school, and was unimpressed by his father's attempt to soften the blow.

'I think Tom might not be very well,' mumbled Peter, looking at the floor.

'He's obviously dead, for God's sake,' said Lawrence.

He then pulled out his homework and briskly got down to his maths, while Peter moped about the kitchen like a lamp whose bulb has gone.

'Come on,' I said. 'It's not as though it's your fault.'

Though I found his inability to address the death issue irritatingly feeble, I did feel a bit sorry for him.

'Actually,' he muttered. 'I think it is. I put them outside.'

'So? They were in their box. It's not as though they ran across the road and were hit by a bus.'

'As they're Australian, I thought they might like a bit of sun.'

Ah.

After a brief interrogation, I established that Tom had been taken outside, left there for two hours in his glass tank and basically grilled.

'Are you saying you didn't know that *glass magnifies heat*?' I said. 'Don't you remember what happened to the *banana*?!'

We left it in the back of the car on a hot day. When we returned an hour later it was black.

'I forgot.'

He hung his head.

That night we checked the care instructions again, and made sure to spray the remaining three phasmids with water more often to maintain humidity. Then term started and we lost another: Jessie, the only female.

The children wanted to bury them in a double grave. They put them in kitchen towels in a hair-dye box and made a cross out of off-cuts of trellis, with their names on. We trooped down the garden with trowels and collectively dug a hole. The box went in and the cross was put in place. No one was sure what to do next.

'We are gathered here today . . . ' began Peter.

'Shut up, Dad,' said Lawrence.

'Goodbye, Tom and Jessie,' said Lydia.

As we walked back to the house, Peter kept saying,

'I'm *so sorry*.'

'That's OK, Dad!' said Lawrence. 'Can we come back next week and dig them up to see what they look like?'

So far, so not particularly traumatic, you may say. But that's just it. Having weathered the loss of the phasmids — the other two died shortly afterwards — Lawrence insisted on a stick insect to replace them in his affections and Lydia began her campaign to get a rabbit.

With her birthday a mere four months away, and using the time-honoured technique of repetition to break down resistance favoured by intelligence services the world over, she began handing out present lists with just one item on them:

'A BUNNY', surrounded by a decorative border made of the words '*PLEASE PLEASE PLEASE PLEASE PLEASE*'.

'We. Are. Not. Getting. You. A. Rabbit,' I repeated firmly, hearing the faint thud as my words, unsupported by any back-up from her father, echoed round the room. Why couldn't he just put his foot down, as opposed to leaving me to be the one who always said No? It was further evidence of his infuriating refusal to deliver any kind of bad news, i.e.

the word 'no', safe in the knowledge that I would do it.

'Why not?' said Lydia. 'I'll look after it.'

'No you won't.'

'Yes I WILL! You don't think I can do ANYTHING.'

'You won't. You'll get bored and I'll have to do it, or Daddy will. And, in any case, there are foxes.'

We have a sizeable population round here; there are now nearly as many foxes in our road as lawyers.

And Peter said,

'We'll see.'

And no, 'We'll see' did not mean 'Never, foolish child!' in his universe as it does in mine. It meant, 'I'll do anything to avoid being unpopular,' which is Peter's guiding philosophy and is in my Top Five reasons for wanting to kill him.

'What *am* I getting for my birthday, then?'

'Something! You'll see.'

'But I don't want anything else.'

I reminded her, several times, that the last time she wrote '*PLEASE PLEASE PLEASE PLEASE PLEASE*' on a present list it was for 'Teksta', the responsive robot horse — it neighs as it whickers as it nuzzles as it does nothing whatsoever, since it had lain abandoned in its box from the day it was handed over to passionate, repeated assurances of 'I promise to love it and play with it FOR EVER'.

She then got a book from the school library called *How to Look After Your Pet Rabbit* and read aloud from it to Peter as they walked home. Even the librarian was in league with them.

' 'Don't necessarily go for the first or the cutest.' That's good advice, isn't it, Daddy?' she was saying, as they came in the door.

'It reminds me', he said, 'of a pamphlet I once got from the Human Resources department on hiring a PA.'

'Don't think I'm distracted by that,' I said. 'Because I'm not.'

Then she started on the section about litter-tray training. I seem to remember doing all this with her and her brother; I felt I'd need a pretty big bribe to go back to it, especially for something that wasn't going to grow up and be voted Form Captain or get any GCSEs.

Over a glass of wine, I complained to my friend Rebecca.

'My sister Jane got a rabbit once,' she sighed. 'It did nothing and ate through everything, including the telephone cables. So we couldn't even fax for help. By the end, we wanted to club it to death.'

I liked the description 'did nothing', like a useless flatmate who repeatedly left his share of the washing-up.

I said to Peter:

'You have to stop promising them things and leaving me to tell them they can't have them.'

'I don't 'promise them things'.'

'You do! Last time you took Lawrence to IKEA you bought him that huge rug!'

'What's that got to do with anything?'

The rug was, to be fair, inanimate.

'It's a perfect example of how you'll do anything to make them think you're marvellous.'

'That's just not true.'

'Why won't you admit it?! Any normal person might take them on a shopping trip and give them a small treat: that means a toy or a bag of sweets, not a bloody £200 rug!'

It goes without saying he's never spent £200 on *me* on the spur of the moment.

'You're just arguing with yourself, you know that?'

'I hate you.'

I flicked through the paper. There was an article about people who rescue ex-battery birds, get them over their post-traumatic cage syndrome, find them good homes and get them laying normally again. A bit like marriage counsellors.

'What do you think about hens?'

'My aunt kept hens.'

'Hens wouldn't be a burden; they'd contribute.'

'I still like Sticky, though,' he said. 'She eats brambles and reproduces asexually.'

He gave me a look which implied I was letting the side down by not doing the same.

'Lydia,' I said. 'Have you considered how amazing Sticky is?'

She nodded and continued her campaign to get a rabbit. Barack Obama was using social networking sites to gather support for his Democratic nomination at the time, and there were definite similarities: the cheery demeanour backed up by immovable determination, fuelled by the almost religious conviction that not just for the lucky candidate but for us all, this outcome would be *right*. And all along, the refrain from Peter of 'We'll see.'

Her tenth birthday was then approaching and she deployed the next stage of her strategy: the refusal to ask for any other present but a rabbit. Not even — not *even* — a game for her Nintendo.

I said, 'No.'

Peter said,

'We'll see.'

'Is this marriage still a democracy?' I demanded. 'Do you even *care* what I think?'

Then a couple of the girls at school who had guinea pigs brought them in, and Lydia was entranced. I asked around. Guinea pigs were *way* cuter than rabbits. They didn't chew through the telephone wires and were easier to pick up, clean out and feed. Was I being unreasonable? Had I done that thing of walling myself into a fixed position on something and refusing to look at it in a new light? After all, I'd said I wasn't going to get married and I'd given way on that. And having children. Both changes of heart had brought me happiness, but on the other hand had also allowed Peter to go around saying,

'You see? I do know what's best for you,' in a way that made me want to rip his head off and kick it down the street.

And there was the small matter of Lydia. If I let her have guinea pigs, she would adore me.

'Maybe guinea pigs will help her be more responsible,' he said. 'After all, leaving toys and sewing all over the floor is one thing, but guinea pigs can't be trodden underfoot, can they? She'll have to look after it.'

'Them.'

'Them.'

We had learned that, like au pairs, they get

depressed on their own. And Lawrence helpfully added that his friend had got his guinea pigs — so adorable! — from a sanctuary, adding an element of philanthropy to the mission.

Lydia could really benefit from this, I began to think. And I made sure she knew it was I who was going to make it happen.

'Can I really have guinea pigs?' said Lydia. 'Really? Really?! Oh Mummy, I love you so much!'

I threw Peter a triumphant look.

'Yes,' I said, 'but I will do no clearing out. I mean, absolutely NONE. Do you understand?'

'Yes, Mummy.'

'If your father wants to, that's his business.'

We went to the sanctuary, a terraced house in Kent containing approximately eighty guinea pigs, and Lydia chose two females, who after much list-making and polling her friends, she then named Cleo and Gemini, like one of those slightly sad singing acts you get in resort hotels:

'Hi, we're Cleo and Gemini, and tonight we'd like to revive for you the golden age of Bucks Fizz . . . '

Lydia fed them and cleaned up their pooh meticulously — using my wok utensil — and after taking her to school I'd sit in the kitchen, reading the paper and talking to them a bit. Nothing deep, just stuff like trying to get them to understand that when there were two pieces of broccoli stalk in their cage, they didn't both have to grab one piece and fight over it. Just, you know, using the mediation skills that Peter thinks I don't have.

First thing in the morning, I noticed, they'd run madly round and round each other, then eat. Then they'd stand still and gaze into the middle distance for a bit. Then they'd fight, then eat again.

'My God,' I told him. 'They're just like us.'

In fact, their psychology was more complex. Gemini, the larger of the two, seemed to be a bit agoraphobic, crouching in the little bunker while Cleo went alone to the food bowl. Then I noticed Gemini was still staying in the little den for long periods, but would suddenly rush out and attack the food bowl with great greed. Gradually, she became more assertive, then really quite fierce. While Cleo would be innocently contemplating her cucumber chunk, Gemini would emerge from the den, shove her out of the way and make off with it. She *pretended* not to be hungry but had forced Cleo into submission and established herself as the dominant female in under a week. It was like the Stanford Prison Experiment.

I told Peter:

'They're like us: the one who seemed really polite at first is actually quite aggressive. She's obviously done that to fool the woman at the sanctuary into offering her to a good home.'

Yet he persisted in trying to spin it as yet another case of 'Steph says No but means Yes' and a further cause for his uncontainable smugness.

'You do like pets,' he said. 'You just hadn't found the right ones.'

'Don't be ridiculous. I'm observing their behaviour and its similarity to ours. As Jane Goodall is to chimpanzees and Dian Fossey was to gorillas, I could be to guinea pigs. It's a scientific thing.'

'Whatever,' he said. 'I always know what you want, before you want it.'

Once again I had supposedly played into his hands: how frustrating.

'I'll say one thing for guinea pigs,' I said. 'They may squabble a lot and pooh anywhere, but at least they're not *smug*. And Lydia knows that *I* let her have them, so now she loves me more.'

'We'll see about that,' he said. 'We'll see.'

22

The Lucky Ones
(*Louise and Bill*)

Louise is married to Bill, a high-ranking consultant at a leading hospital: his job title takes up three lines on an email. He's also good-looking, charming and self-deprecatingly amusing; the first time I met him, I just melted away at his hilarious story of trying to buy a really cool classic car and ending up with quite a bad one. (Peter, of course, nodded sagely throughout.) He also takes the kids swimming — and even occasionally camping, so Louise can get some time to herself. Basically, he's the man you'd trample your best friend into the dirt to get.

So I am quite surprised when she says life with him isn't utterly marvellous.

'Er, isn't that exactly what people say to you about Peter?' she says, with commendable restraint.

'But Bill really *is* lovely. Isn't he?'

She rolls her eyes, and I realize I'm about to bond with someone who will have come closer than anyone to knowing what it's like

151

to be married to Peter. For she too is lumbered with a Paragon.

'Still,' I say. 'Obviously it's going to be quite a challenge for you to actually tell me what's wrong with him. I mean, bar the occasional irritation.'

She looks at me almost blankly for a moment; it's just so hard not to fall into the trap of believing in the Myth of the Superspouse.

I'm sitting in her warm, clean kitchen, marvelling over the fact that although she had a third child just over a year ago, there are no dreadful sticky patches and it doesn't smell.

'Obviously,' I say, 'he's very likeable.'

'That's one of the things I hate about him,' she says. 'Everybody likes him!'

'I know the nightmare of *that*,' I say.

Could I have found the one woman in London who *understands*?

'He's the Voice of Reason,' she continues, 'which is annoying. He's a pacifist, which is annoying.'

'Do you argue, though?'

Peter's technique is often to refuse to engage, so he can say that thing that makes me absolutely furious:

'You're just arguing with yourself.'

'We argue about politics. Well, those are the more sensible arguments. The children will quite often come down and say, 'Are you getting a divorce?''

'Oh no!'

Do Lawrence and Lydia feel this too? I feel a stab of guilt. But Louise isn't beating herself up.

'He's learned that I'm very fiery. I shoved him once during an argument on holiday, and one of the kids became hysterical. It was nothing, really. But she thought it was, you know, The End.'

'I can imagine.'

I haven't shoved Peter — yet, but by God I've wanted to.

'Because I'm very emotional, I can't always explain *why* I hold a certain view. Because he can express his views more — skilfully — he feels his position is more valid. He doesn't put me down or anything, I just know he feels he's right. Also I rant and rave. I often feel inadequate because of my terrible education. He'll laugh at my lack of knowledge of historical events. He's incredibly bright and that's annoying sometimes.'

Bill is next door watching television. At this point he comes in to reclaim his slippers, which she's borrowed. He sounds almost stern as he says,

'Can I have them back, please?'

But it's nothing by my standards; it

wouldn't even show up on an infra-red anger map of the house.

'Would you say you're more confident than Louise, because of being more educated?' I ask him.

'Well, I can still remember all my Latin declensions. I used to go to bed reciting them.'

She rolls her eyes.

'Sexy!' I say.

'When I was at *school*.'

He gives one of his loud, generous laughs and goes back to the rugby.

'Well, I'm sorry,' I say. 'I think Peter is far more difficult.'

However, I'm in no mood to argue; I'm so fascinated by talking to someone else with a Perfect Husband that I feel quite elated. It's really comforting, like finding someone who has the same chronic, non-fatal but intermittently debilitating condition, like asthma or too many relatives.

Louise's next complaint I've heard again and again. I cannot guess what the evolutionary advantage could possibly be, yet it really is extraordinarily common in men.

'If he's lost something, he doesn't look for it properly. He says, 'I can't see the cheese in the fridge.' But he doesn't move anything to find it. If I say, 'Can you get me the blue dish from the drawer?' he'll just peer in and say,

'It's not there.' He won't lift up one thing to find it.'

'Ah well, that's your Y-chromosome, you see.'

OK, I have no medical basis for this. Luckily Bill is in the other room and can't hear.

'Lawrence says he can't find his blazer. But there it is — hanging behind Lydia's coat.'

'Or the other day, when he was making his own lunch — sort of — he moaned:

'Where's the olive oil?'

'On the counter.'

'Where's the pesto?'

'There on the counter also. You've got these balls — '' I said.

'Mum!'

'' — called eyes. You use them to *see*.''

'I mean, the counter had virtually nothing else on it. It's like walking into the middle of Paris and saying, 'Where's the Eiffel Tower?''

I don't tell Louise that Peter almost always *can* find things because once again, it makes him sound perfect, and there comes a point where I just can't stand it.

She goes on:

'He's not practical *at all*.'

'Blimey,' I say. 'He's not a surgeon, is he? Because that would be funny — I mean in an awful way. Obviously.'

No: he does something very complicated in genetics.

'But I have to do *everything*. Flat packs!'

While she's talking, I'm thinking: hang on. There are very few people in the entire human race who can do flat packs. They're like people with perfect pitch: benign mutations. Peter, needless to say, is one. And here we have another. And she's a *woman*.

'Hey, that's amazing . . . ' I begin. But she's moved on.

'He's currently in charge of our finances. But we keep getting overdrawn. But if I complain he'll say, 'You do it then.' And at the moment, I don't want to!'

But at least she accepts that if she doesn't want to look after the finances, she'll have to put up with the odd overdraft; you can't have it both ways.

'I couldn't bear anyone else having control of the money.' I say. 'And luckily Peter is innumerate.'

The first time we got a mortgage I explained it to him, and I could see his eyes glazing over like Father Dougal's when Father Ted[1] used toy cows to try to get him to understand the difference between 'Small' and 'Far Away'. I recently taught the children

---

[1] The excellent Channel 4 sitcom.

156

Twenty-one and whereas they got it straight away, Lawrence displaying an instinctive flair for gambling with cards that was actually quite worrying, Peter took *ages* to add up his totals: a bit sad when you think that you only start with a hand of two. He also quite often folded because he thought he had twenty-two, when he actually had a perfectly good hand of nineteen or twenty. Or even, on one ridiculous occasion, twenty-one. If I was that bad at maths would I be as smug as he is? I don't *think* so.

Louise goes on:

'He has no sense of time. If we have to be somewhere at eight, he'll think we can leave at eight.'

Ah, the old Bendy Time Syndrome, like Jon going on Multimap at the moment they're meant to leave. Why is that? Whenever someone asks him how long it takes us to get somewhere, Peter always says, 'Twenty minutes'. It's part of his rose-tinted vision of the world, that everything takes twenty minutes. When we lived in north London, and people asked where his sister lived, he'd say, 'Oh, Herne Hill: it's twenty minutes away,' when in fact it was at least forty. It used to irritate me beyond belief. He seemed to regard my peculiar penchant for — er, reality — as bizarrely pessimistic, as if I wanted to keep saying how difficult life was, with its terrible forty-minute journeys. But that's how long it took! I mean, you don't say, 'I have a brother in Mumbai: it's an hour,' do you? Bloody hell.

Louise is trying to find more things wrong with Bill, but quite honestly she's struggling.

'I don't care that he doesn't cook, but when he does — the FUSS! It's like a scientific experiment. And he uses every pan and utensil. Now I generally ask him not to: it's not worth it.'

This is another complaint I've heard about husbands, that they use everything down to the last spoon. I assume it comes from having never had to wash up. Having said that, Peter hardly ever cooks, which suits me fine as I love doing it and it gets me out of a ton of other household tasks. What's more, he often cleans up after *I've* cooked. I suppose now I've told you that, you'll think he really is Perfect and this whole book will have been for nothing.

I decide not to share this with Louise. We haven't been friends that long. Instead, I introduce a source of stress that — through no fault of Peter's, or should I say, no credit to him — doesn't apply in his case: inlaws.

'So tell me about Bill's family. Isn't that one of the greatest causes of stress in marriage? The in-laws?'

'Well, they are unable to deal with conflict of any kind,' she explains. 'I often argue with his brother, about ideological things, you know, and they think that's *terrible*. As if you just can't disagree.'

Bill reappears at this point and she asks him for his view of *her* family. He laughs — warmly.

'They never let the facts get in the way of the truth. They'll say something like, 'There are 200,000 teenage pregnancies every year in London alone.' And it's not true at all!'

'We're just using that figure to make the general point.'

'But it's complete rubbish!'

She shrugs wearily and he smiles broadly as he goes back into the other room. She gazes critically after him.

'He shouts when he's watching it. Really loudly. And during Wimbledon, I got really cross.'

I listen hard, but hear no shouting.

'I'm afraid he really isn't that bad,' I say.

And she says,

'Sorry', as if I'm blaming her for having a good marriage, whereas I'm glad to have met a fellow sufferer, another recruit for my club of women married to men everyone thinks are perfect.

But what I'm also trying to do is learn from her, this aim being based on my Life Plan, that if I sit in a room with, or near, people who are good at something, that skill or knowledge will somehow magically transmit itself and I will improve. Because I have a feeling that, despite his marvellousness, these two really are OK. Well, all right, Louise clearly doesn't fly into a temper as easily as I do, so the marriage is already at a huge advantage right there.

Before I go, I remember an observation she made on a previous occasion that struck me as very perceptive. She was talking about a woman she knows who 'can't go out' to do anything for herself, such as get a haircut, because she always has the children and supposedly can't ever leave them with her husband. Louise and I agreed that we couldn't understand this, although I know it's by no means unique. I knew a girl years ago whose husband did nothing at all around the house or with the children, and he wasn't even in work. She'd go off to her two jobs, trailing the toddlers behind her, and he'd go to the pub. Eventually she divorced him and married a grown-up.

So why can't this one do the same? Go out, I mean, not get divorced.

'You just go, 'Here are the children: I'm off

to get my hair done,'' I say.

'Well, quite,' says Louise. 'That's more or less what I told her, and she said, 'Oh, you're so lucky with Bill.' And I thought, what a coincidence: that the 'lucky' women are always the demanding ones like us.'

By God, she's right. Admittedly there's a difference between demanding and impossible. But she may have hit on something. The really good men often coincidentally turn out to be the ones whose wives are really clear about what they want. And there, my friends, is a bit of genuine marital wisdom. I'd say it's more than worth the cover price. Try it, and if you don't find it improves your marriage, Bill will give you your money back.

23

Sex, Attachment and Nibbles

While attempting to find out how some people — including myself — manage to stay married, I have a wonderful stroke of luck. An invitation arrives in the post to the Society of Analytic Psychology, one of the leading training and research centres for what is properly called psychoanalytic psychotherapy. That's the old-fashioned kind, where you sit in a room with a therapist who doesn't say anything until you do, and it costs a lot.

But it's not to get shrunk, as my dad used to put it. (He actually used to say, cheerily, as he left, 'I'm off to get my head shrunk.') I've been invited to attend a discussion and the launch of a snappy little volume called *Sex, Attachment and Couple Psychotherapy*. Attachment, in case you haven't had millions of years of therapy, is what shrinks call love. I'm not sure why I've been sent this, mind you. Possibly when I *was* being shrunk, years ago, they kept my name on file as someone who was likely to have to come back. They might even have special software for it now, that pings off an email after ten or twenty years, helpfully asking if your life has fallen apart again, a bit like renewing a damp course. Except of course without the guarantee.

One thing I like about the invitation is that it mentions a discussion followed by 'drinks and nibbles', nibbles being one of those words I usually associate with PTA meetings, or parties where people suddenly try to sell you jewellery. It's not a word I would expect to come across in the context of serious delvings into the psyche. I mean, you can't imagine Sigmund Freud inviting anyone round for nibbles, although he did have a sense of humour, despite the impression you get from *Jokes and Their Relation to the Unconscious* — a book I read in vain looking for a laugh.

The thing is, when you start getting into this realm, you start thinking like a therapist and suddenly nothing seems accidental. I would say that whoever typed 'nibbles' on to the invitation is likely to be orally fixated, which is good, because it's likely to mean there'll be plenty of them. Nibbles, I mean, not orally fixated admin staff, though that would also be comforting. A conference for orally fixated therapists would certainly be worth going to because it might just be one really enormous, 48-hour buffet.

The other reason I'm here, talking of food, is that one of the speakers is Susie Orbach, author of the brilliant *Fat is a Feminist Issue*. We can gorge on the nibbles and then deconstruct our motives for doing so. Or, in Susie's case, not gorge, as I see that since the publication of that groundbreaking work she has not put on so much as a gram, which is perhaps to be expected of someone who understands why women eat too much, or too little, better than anyone on earth. She is the only professionally qualified, practising shrink in the UK who is also a household name, and for one very good reason: she can communicate with any kind of audience. So I will be able to hear her speak, have nibbles and even learn something about relationships for this book. I set off keenly and even a bit early.

Hampstead has more therapists per square metre than anywhere on earth — possibly even than New York, though they stack them higher there — and having travelled from deepest south London, I am running late. When you're late for a session, your therapist inevitably spends at least the first ten of your extremely costly fifty minutes speculating as to why. Explanations such as 'the bus was late' or 'my car broke down' do not wash. Everything you do in relation to your session is deemed significant. Just how significant depends on how orthodox the therapist is. The really strict Freudian ones consider all instances of lateness to be acts influenced by your subconscious, including acts of war, whereas the less traditional ones will give you some leeway. They're willing to accept that buses can be late or cars can break down, and not insist that you've created a traffic jam or sabotaged your own clutch to avoid discussing your feelings about your father. Mind you, they still won't let you make up the extra time.

So it is in this spirit of nostalgia and mild nervousness that I scuttle down the main road clutching my printed off Multimap, press the doorbell, and am directed down a corridor of identical closed doors by a woman who seems unable to be clear about precisely which one I should open. Immediately the old anxiety comes back, mixed with feelings of helplessness, as I try first one door then another, while the woman doesn't move or gesture but just says, 'Not that one' each time. I hate making mistakes and *really* hate being late, and bursting into a roomful of people all listening to a speaker who has already begun speaking, I do not relish. When I go in, will forty therapists all turn round and pick apart my attempt to blame the

Northern Line? I remind myself that it's an imperfect world and I am a grown-up, ish, and enter the room confidently, mouthing a random 'sorry' to the first person I see.

It's not a very big room, just an office, with lots of textbooks on shelves all round, and a couple of desks. The desks have been pushed to one side to make room for rows of seats, which are packed in. Susie Orbach, who is speaking, is on one of the three chairs at the far end, with Christopher Clulow, who is the editor of the book they are launching, and another professional, David Hewison. There is a friendly atmosphere, which is a relief, as being the only non-therapist there I'm instantly overwhelmed by a combination of bravado and guilt, like a choirboy who's snuck into the other side of the confessional. What trade secrets will I be party to, that I can share with the outside world? Will I find out why couples have problems, and in so many cases, split up?

'It seems that couples psychotherapists often don't talk about sex,' one of the men is saying, I think Clulow. 'Even at a seminar specifically about sex, they talked about anything else but!'

There is a knowing but restrained giggle from the audience. What better way to address our discomfort about sex, as a culture, than by saying that even at sex therapy seminars no one talks dirty? It reminds me of a sketch I once saw on the show *Smack the Pony* about a squeamish doctor. The doctor is cowering by her desk and the patient, who obviously has some kind of gynaecological problem, gets on the couch and says, 'Well, aren't you going to examine me?'

And the doctor leans over, pokes her really, really quickly on the tummy with one finger and then sort of leaps away. It's even funnier than a chain-smoking doctor, though that wasn't a sketch but — in the seventies — my actual GP. She would diagnose you through thick clouds of smoke, puffing away. It's amazing any of us made it out of the surgery alive.

Anyhow, I am pondering the numerous ways in which people avoid the subject of sex when I notice a table at the far end of the room, near the speakers, with a stack of transparent plastic cups and two bowls of crisps. Hmm, if these are the aforementioned 'nibbles', I'm not tremendously impressed. Lunch feels like days ago, and dinner is another two hours away at least.

Just then an arpeggio of police sirens go off, followed by the door buzzer, which is surprising because if there's one golden rule I remember from having therapy it's that during a session they never, *ever* answer the door. Over the course of five years my therapist's doorbell went once. I think it was someone delivering a package — a really big carton of tissues is what I imagined — but she let it be known that it was an aberration, not to be taken lightly. She even apologized, taking responsibility for the interruption. Therapists are very dedicated and don't like to divert their attention from their patients. Put it this way: if you're ever driving through Hampstead and break down without your mobile, don't bother trying any houses to borrow the phone. I shouldn't imagine they're much bothered by Jehovah's Witnesses, either. Maybe *they* just avoid the area altogether, which makes quite a strong argument for putting up a brass plate on your house saying '*Dr Shrinkoffsky* — *Psychoanalyst*' which would be like garlic to vampires.

I squeeze into the tight rows of chairs and get settled. Now Susie is praising the book, but I miss a bit of what she says when the man behind me starts coughing. Then I notice a weird, intermittent humming.

'The society we live in has become highly sexualized, but de-eroticized,' says Susie.

'Hmm, yes, yes,' says the woman beside me to herself, apparently without realizing she's

168

saying it out loud.

'We don't disagree on this, do we?' says Susie to Hewison.

'Well, it was good for me!' he says, and gets quite a big laugh. The laugh takes time to build, as if the therapists have to reset themselves to take in the joke. She moves on:

'Sex can be exciting and, dare I say in front of you, dirty.'

This provokes nervous titters — again, something you don't associate with professionals. I miss a bit, and then hear:

'We don't celebrate our daughters finding their clitorises,' says Susie. 'Their genital development.'

Ooh. Suddenly I want to drop my pen so I can bend down and hide in case she spots me, as my mother told me they used to at school, when they had to read out verses from the Bible. They'd drop their pens or suddenly get a dry throat when it came to their turn if their verse contained a rude word, e.g. 'loins' or 'womb'.

Actually I totally agree about the clitoris being worth celebrating — certainly far more so than Hallowe'en or the nine hundredth anniversary of Westminster Abbey, though I can't really visualize how. Possibly it was first discovered by someone in Babylon or Ancient Greece, yet I can't see it being the subject of one of those popular science bestsellers, like *Longitude* or *The Map that Changed the World*. And massively deserving though it undoubtedly is, it does rather have a ring about it of the feminist 'Exploring Your Vulva' workshops of the seventies. On which point, if you missed the seventies and want to experience the magic — but without the power cuts, strikes and patchwork maxi-skirts — read Lisa Alther's *Kinflicks*, in which the heroine and her friends hold a consciousness-raising weekend which includes a 'See Your Own Cervix' workshop and a finale in which one of the group is electrocuted by her own vibrator. The nearest thing to a Celebration of the Clitoris Finding I've ever heard of in Real Life was a Pink Party, which a friend of a friend, very feminist (and lesbian), inflicted on her newly menstruating daughter. History does not record whether they are still speaking, but the friend who told me about it, though herself feminist (and lesbian), did hold it up as a benchmark of feminist looniness and it became our shorthand for describing the nonsensical extremes perpe-trated by the 'wimmin' of that decade. I suppose, though, it might come in handy as something I could threaten Lydia with, as I do Lawrence with the promise that if he doesn't pick up his games kit and help clear the table, I will come to collect him from school wailing, '*Lawwence, I wuv you!*' across the playground in anguished tones.

The buzzer goes again. The coughing man is now whispering, none too quietly, to the woman next to him. What is it with men and their inability to whisper? Now Susie is talking about a 'double hole'. I'm pretty sure this is metaphorical, so I must have missed a bit. She makes another good point:

'There must be some incompatibility between sex relationships and care-giving relationships.'

She has again hit the nail on the head; this split is absolutely key when women become mothers. She adds that the early part of parenthood can definitely hinder sex, or even stop it altogether, something I've always thought isn't recognized nearly enough. I remember the really quite weird feeling provoked by breastfeeding, that the activity was disconcertingly similar to something that normally goes with sex, yet — *Jeez!* The man behind takes out a blister pack of some pills or something *really, really* crackly which he pops out, or folds, ve-ry slow-ly. *I'm trying to concentrate! Could you please shut the fuck up?*

The coughing and whispering man, talking woman, police sirens and door buzzer seem to me an apt illustration of the distractions that conspire to prevent couples — particularly parents — from having sex. Obviously, children are the main hindrance. Now that ours are older, we can farm them out to their friends for sleepovers and get them out of the way like that, but being that bit older we're even more likely than before to doze off before we can do anything. It's pathetic, but there you are. Mind you, now that they're nearly teenagers, they're starting to become incapable of getting up in the mornings but we still wake up horribly early, so weekends are once again looking possible. I just have to watch out that I don't do anything fatal to my knees. I've already had to rule out some of the more — to me — exotic positions, but even the old missionary has its pitfalls as without the exact thickness of pillow behind me I can end up cricking my neck. Still, even if Peter doesn't achieve a shag, he does at least get some exercise running downstairs to get the ice pack.

Clulow invites contributions. A woman stands up and says that a male patient of hers claimed to have had an orgasm while having his hair washed at the hairdresser's. There is a stunned silence followed by a gasp. No one asks for the name of the hairdresser.

Now I hear a loud rustling behind me as

the whispering man starts leafing through the book that's being discussed. The woman next to me continues to mutter responses. Then she stands up and tries to steer the debate round to a discussion about class. Clulow makes a nifty reference to 'Who's on top', but surprisingly doesn't get a laugh. The whispering man and the woman next to him are now openly conducting a conversation.

The discussion moves on to celibacy, and the muttering woman is off again:

'Mm, mm, interesting.'

A psychosexual counsellor says,

'We talk about sex all day long, every day, for hours on end!'

Well, yes, she presumably would do. She also makes a reference to an earlier comment about penis envy, which would have been before I came in — both literally and historically, since it's such outdated nonsense. I've *never* met a woman who wished she had a penis, except possibly in order to earn 23 per cent more salary or take up two seats for no reason on the tube.

My train of thought is interrupted for the final time by an odd sound from the landing, either of champagne corks popping or someone being spanked with an old-fashioned carpet beater; we haven't covered S & M. Clulow says it's time to have a drink, and before we all rise, the psychosexual counsellor seems to sum it all up:

'The woman often wants to connect through conversation; the man *always* wants to connect through sex.'

And there you have it. She's only talking about her patients but I'm sure that, if asked, most women would say of their marriages that they don't talk enough, and most men that they don't shag enough. And as we all stand, Susie delivers the punchline:

'How do you cure a Jewish nymphomaniac?'

She leaves a perfectly timed pause.

'Marry her.'

24

Room Service, and Hold the Sex

Two-thirty a.m. I'm awake, having had a bad dream about people driving cars through the house. This is what comes of marrying a man who takes an interest in Formula 1; I used to find myself automatically flicking to the motoring programmes on the TV pages and now his hobbies have pervaded not only my external viewing but my dreams as well. I'm quite tolerant of cars and anything engine-related but frankly this is a bit much.

Three-thirty a.m. Now he's awake as well. 'What are you doing?!'

I say:

'Trying to get back to sleep! I had a bad dream about cars — which is your fault.'

'Well, keep still!'

All I have to do is turn over or pull the duvet up two centimetres to cover my shoulders, and he complains. Whereas he not only snores, but in between snoring breathes REALLY LOUDLY — so that it's like being woken every two hours by Darth Vader. But not in a sexy, black-cloaked, galaxy-ruling sort of way.

'You're so annoying!'

I snuggle my head on to his shoulder.

'Blimey!' he says. 'Did you just fart?'

'Um, possibly.'

For some reason I've lately had a bit of a problem in that department. No wait, hang on, so has he!

'Well, don't waft it around.'

'I'm not!'

'Keep still.'

'Look,' I say, 'just stop twitching about, will you, and keep the duvet down.'

'I am.'

At that point a particularly pungent vapour wafts up through the fibres. 'There is something awful in the nearness it brings,' said George Eliot of marriage, and the words of the great Victorian novelist are very much in my mind as he says,

'Oh God, our farts have mingled . . . '

And people wonder why some couples who've been together for two decades don't have as much sex.

I think in our case the problem is also a paradox. One, we're best friends. And two, we're best friends.

Quite obviously, if you're still mates after all this time, who tell each other your hopes and fears, share your highs and lows, that's wonderful. We really do talk. On the other hand, even the word 'mates' is already rather draining the atmosphere of its erotic potential. And if we've come to realize after twenty years that we've both developed a lot of characteristics of the blokes in *Men Behaving Badly*, I know also that I'm bound to have lost, as a result, a bit of my feminine mystique. The sex is absolutely great when we have it, but we have somewhat fallen down on the seduction front.

He goes downstairs to make us some tea.

'This isn't so much a marriage,' he says, 'as a dorm.'

And I know he's right, because quite apart from creating all those smells, we go to the next stage of the Best Mates Continuum, which is to tell each other whom we fancy, though not in a creepy, Open Marriage sort of way:

'Peter, I sometimes have sexual desires for other men.'

'Darling, that's completely natural and I am not at all threatened by it.'

No, we just sometimes tell each other who we'd like to shag. And just occasionally, I'm so relaxed that I forget that he actually is my husband, and it sort of slips over into what I'd confide to a friend.

'Guess what, I met this bloke today I really wanted to f — Oh, look! An original DB5!'[1]

Except I don't even do that very often, because it only happens quite rarely. After twenty years and God knows how many arguments, we both appear to have been faithful. Is it lack of opportunity, or lack of nerve? And should we be proud of that, at least?

A number of questions arise. Since being mates with your spouse dissipates your mystique, could it — paradoxically — protect you from infidelity at the same time? I mean, who would betray their best friend?

Actually, it turns out, quite a lot of people. That particular nightmare features in the problem pages surprisingly frequently. I even know someone it happened to, though I am still amazed and baffled, since to me the very familiarity of your best friend's husband, the sheer mundanity of them, if you like, surely automatically puts them out of the running. I love the husbands of my closest friends — I don't think we'd be quite so close if I didn't — but I've seen them too often first thing in the morning, or holding sicky babies, to think of them in a remotely sexual way. If you've

---

[1] Note to female readers: the Aston Martin driven by Sean Connery in *Goldfinger*.

ever been in the vicinity of a man who's unshaven, with awful breath, and dressed in one of those dingy dressing gowns they seem to have such a fondness for, there's no way you could want to shag him. If you do, that's just weird, like fancying your brother, or your doctor. And yes, I do know people do, and my late stepfather, who was a GP, attested to this when he returned from house calls to women with indeterminate symptoms who wore black lace negligees in the middle of the day. But to have rude fantasies about someone who's looked down your throat, or zapped your warts, or — God forbid — examined your bottom, is just *too* bizarre. I know I'm not the most relaxed person on the planet when it comes to these things; I have to pass the nurse who gave me my last smear test on the way to school most mornings, and it's taken me about two terms to perfect a kind of neutral, meaningless nod. Luckily she's really tall, so my nether regions are at least at some distance from her consciousness. But if she was a man — blurgh!

That's why I found the reticence of those therapists so reassuring, because I find the whole idea of sex a bit strange already. Even in my forties, with the man I'm actually married to, I still can't quite believe it's legal.

And it's not as though we do anything *weird*, either.

Some people do, of course. For example, they drive to deserted lay-bys to have sex in front of strangers. Sex in cars I get — I mean kind of, though not with my back. I've fiddled a few times in cars, mainly as a teenager. But grown-ups? In a *lay-by*? What's wrong with a nice hotel — with a bed and sheets?

As they have for the last fifty years, magazines still urge you to 'Spice Up Your Marriage', advice that's likely nowadays to involve pole dancing — and what woman wants to stand next to something that thin? I'm more comfortable with the version from fifty years ago, when it meant cooking paella.

I *try* to be more uninhibited. I tried to buy a porn film from HMV once, or I strongly considered attempting it. I got as far as the shelves and sort of leaned towards them. There was no one around who knew me, no other parents from school, or teachers, or whoever I feared might be lurking in the basement of HMV in the middle of a weekday. I heard of a woman who once knocked a whole shelf of porn videos on to the floor in a shop in Soho and looked up to see her son's class teacher standing there. I can't handle the idea of anyone even seeing me looking, even strangers. And then after all that a friend of mine said disparagingly.

'HMV?! That's not even real porn!'

Yes, but we've got to start somewhere. I was on M & S online buying a dressing gown the other day, and the women's were all covered in horrible patterns or the colour of raw chicken, so I looked at the men's; they were nice and plain. Out of curiosity, I watched the little video of how to wear the dressing gown once you've bought it — which even for really undomesticated men struck me as superfluous. It consisted of a very attractive guy, in an unfeasibly tidy room, smirking out of a window while glancing down at a pink newspaper that has to have been the *Financial Times*. I watched it four times — sad, you may say. But there are women who might be aroused by that, would want to whip off the dressing gown and scrutinize his bonus.

I know, I know: instead of doing that I should have been ordering some rude films. But I can't work up the nerve to do that either; all our net activity is recorded on the servers and I just don't like the idea of anyone in the Government finding out that I once bought a DVD called *Beverly Hills Cock*.[1] And I certainly don't understand

---

[1] This is a real title. I didn't order it.

people who want to film themselves. A guy I went out with years ago once showed me a homemade porn film given to him by a mate. And though it was clearly done with the full consent of the woman, all I could think was: God, what unflattering lighting. The lighting wasn't a problem for him, of course.

Would I have an affair? *Could* I? I'd like someone to *want* to sleep with me, but I'd never be able to go through with it. Lucy's right about the fear of anyone else seeing my tummy. Even glancing at myself unintentionally makes me uncomfortable — something that has got far worse with age. When you look in a mirror you generally sort of lift yourself up, don't you? Recently I was in a building where the only loo was wheelchair friendly. And unlike every other disabled lavatory I've ever seen, it had a mirror — taking up pretty much the whole of one wall. My bottom isn't even that big, but I was so horrified by the sight of it — and my thighs, spread out like mounds of tripe — that I had to pee with my head turned away. Before Peter, I had a very nice boyfriend called Des who lived briefly in one of those flats designed by people who think fitted wardrobes with mirrored doors are incredibly 'aspirational'. Whenever I came to stay, he had to hang a sheet over them, otherwise we couldn't do anything. And I was in my twenties, with quite an OK figure, so it wasn't due to body dysmorphia: more mirror dislikia.

But in any case, I can't imagine having that sort of intimacy with another man, let alone seeing a strange willy after all this time — which would just be horrendous. I think it's more the paraphernalia I'd be interested in, the stuff that goes *with* an affair.

For example, hotel rooms. Hotel rooms are definitely sexy. Supposedly it's the anonymity: not having to be reminded of your normal life, and who you really are. And I think that's true. Women in particular find it hard to compartmentalize, and are apt to be distracted at home by a child's sock or a dusty corner they may have missed. The other attraction for me is room service. I had a fling with a guy once in another city which involved quite a bit of late-night hotel-room eating, with the incredible exhilaration that comes from not having to clear up. I think, now, it's really that and the fresh sheets — so much nicer than a frayed duvet cover with pen marks, that I find enticing. So maybe let's not bother with the sex and just order room service.

Because really, how likely is it that the sex is going to be better? Speaking for myself,

183

very *unlikely*. I've taken quite a while to get to this point; I can't face starting again. It's not like wiring, where everything is in roughly the same arrangement whichever house you're in. Also, it's hugely subjective: how fast, slow, up, down. It can take years to train a man up. By the time you've got it the way you want it, it's monogamy anyway. With room service at least someone brings you what you want and while you enjoy it, gets out of your way. I get quite a lot of excitement from reading a new menu. So, food in the company of an attractive man — no, food and conversation; he'd have to be able to talk. That would be my ideal affair, basically: a series of discussions in hotel rooms, over meals.

Anyhow, even if someone *did* want to have an affair with me, I wouldn't be able to go through with it even if the sex was good and my tummy was flat; even if I *did* have the nerve and *could* stand the shame of being discovered. And even if I suddenly developed the skills of a really good liar. Whenever I speculate about it, I always imagine sending a rude text to the wrong person, hurriedly pressing the name next to theirs, having stupidly chosen someone with the same initials as the IT man or the piano teacher.

But it's also because I just know, the way I know when Lydia desperately wants another cuddly animal that she can't possibly live without, that the excitement would be very short-lived and the guilt absolutely *huge*. But the even bigger obstacle, the biggest obstacle of all, would be that, being a woman, I'd be unable to do it without telling my best friend. And my best friend is you-know-who.

So fidelity it is, and I can't even take any credit for having superior morals.

25

There Are Only So Many Plots
(*Judith and Roger*)

It's all very well *you* being too scaredy-pants to be unfaithful, you may be thinking, but what about him? I've asked him a few times if he thinks he could, and he always says no — of course — and I say,

'Well, if you do ever meet anyone who wants to discuss the decline of British industry while taking their clothes off, good luck to you, old man.'

OK, he doesn't talk about that *all* the time. Still, if anyone did show an interest in him, part of me would be rather flattered.

If any of our friends are 'carrying on', as they used to call it, they're hiding it pretty well. We did know one chap years ago who was spotted with another woman at a hotel, his mistake being choosing the same place he'd taken the family to the year before. And we know couples, of course, who are divorced. But there is only one pair we've known throughout the process of infidelity, break-up and divorce.

Peter knew Judith well before he and I met. She and her husband Roger got together when they were both seventeen, and were married at twenty, which seems unimaginably young. She is now sixty, although she looks and sounds — without being at all self-conscious about it — an awful lot younger. Hers is the generation that came between my mother's, who were brought up to view marriage as their only goal, and mine, who expected to have not just family and careers, but absolute parity with men. And they didn't sit around examining their ambitions and motives all the time. For example, I ask, 'How did you come to the decision to have children?'

They have a boy and a girl, Dan and Chloe.

And she says, 'We never discussed it.'

It seems extraordinary, when you think of the amount people bang on about parenthood nowadays and how incredibly seriously it's all taken, not to mention the endless analysis of whether we're all *happy*.

'I think the ambivalence came in when he was about forty,' she says. 'He said he wasn't sure about his life and our life together and that he was 'staring into a black hole'. I'd got a new job, and was earning more money than him, and Dan was becoming a young man.

Maybe it had something to do with that.'

'You *think* . . . ?'

Actually, who knows?

'He became very preoccupied with work, and kept making long work phone calls. And of course Linda was his PA.'

As my mother always says, there are only so many plots.

'Then we went on holiday with some friends, and he was constantly on the phone.'

Bear in mind this was about sixteen years ago and pre mobiles; he had to walk to the village phone box each time with his pockets full of five-franc coins.

'It seems laughably obvious now, but you can't see the juggernaut coming towards you,' she says. 'I worked with a guy once who came into the office, slammed his briefcase down on the desk and said he'd finally worked out why the mechanic had been up and down to his house for six months, fixing his wife's car.

'Six months!' he kept saying. 'Six months!''

'It was awful, the feeling of utter stupidity.'

I've just remembered I worked with someone who had that experience too. Would I be any smarter? Would Peter? But as I said before, he wouldn't need to be because I am such a terrible liar.

She says:

'I didn't want to confront him because I

didn't want to be disliked. I didn't want to be abandoned. But finally I said, 'Look, is there somebody else?' and he said,

'Ooh, no!' And I just *knew* there was. I should have said, 'Just fuck off, then! Go!' But he kept saying he just 'needed more space'.'

More space? You'd think people would come up with fresher clichés. I think there should be a rule that, every decade, they expire. In the eighties you should no longer have been able to say you were working late at the office, and in the nineties you certainly shouldn't have been allowed to 'need more space'. If Peter ever says he needs more space he can get the tent out and go and live in the garden.

But I'm avoiding what it must feel like to realize that the man you've loved and lived with for well over twenty years, since you were practically a bloody child, is slipping away from you. And there's nothing you can do — particularly if he repeatedly denies there's anything wrong. Peter and I always say we'd tell each other, and maybe everyone says that, but is it different once you're seriously involved with someone else?

Gradually the picture for Judith began to become clearer and clearer, like those Magic Eye images that look like a jumble of dots until you focus in a certain way and see a yacht or a horse.

'A friend said she'd seen his car parked in so-and-so road. And I found out that Linda lived there.'

Erk!

'And still Roger went on and on denying it until a friend said to me, 'Just grab the reins: you don't want someone living in the house who doesn't want to be there.' So I told him to help to make things work between us or go. We told the kids Dad needed some time to himself to cope with pressures at work — which was a cop out, but we both wanted to protect them.'

Hmm. I guess you don't know what you'd say until it happens to you. I'd probably say something like:

'Dad's shagging someone else, the fucking, shitting, arseholing bastard, so I'm kicking him out and I hope he dies a slow, horrible death.' But then I tend to be swayed by the mood of the moment.

'I felt embarrassed that this was happening to me. The day he left was awful, obviously: Chloe sat on the sofa and cried. She was fourteen. Dan, who was more outwardly unaffected, made us tea. And coming home to the empty house was hard. A friend advised me to get a gas fire and to put it on as soon as I came in to make the house more welcoming.'

It's a very evocative image, and really helps me imagine how it might feel, since I'm still at the stage where an empty house is — briefly — a cause for celebration, a rare opportunity to read the paper or put the TV on without Lydia wresting the remote from my hand and forcing us all to watch the Top 40 Singing And Writhing Scantily Clad Women.

'Our circle of friends was amazed. A sort of shock wave went round them, that it was us of all people. Oddly enough, I recovered more quickly than they did. They took longer to come to terms with it.'

But that makes a kind of sense, because of all the ripples. You don't just lose a marriage; socially, a whole structure goes down. As Nora Ephron says in her book *Heartburn*, losing her husband also damaged the foursome with their best friends:

'Two of us liked white meat and two of us liked dark meat and together we made a chicken.'

You miss being that chicken. And besides, if Judith and Roger can't make it, they must have thought, what hope is there for the rest of us? People start to worry, to doubt their own certainties. They were like the Twin

Towers: people suddenly realized the divorce terror could strike anywhere.

'After a while I became quite clear-sighted; I'd gone through a sort of pain barrier and survived. I ensured the kids saw their dad. I just made sure that whenever he came round to see them, I went out. And some time later he said, 'I didn't realize when I left you that I'd lose you.''

Oh, come on!

'Perhaps he thought he could carry on having it all.'

Perhaps he really did. After all, quite a few men do. Not only did he miss her, when he had a child with Linda, he apparently realized what he'd done: exchanged one scenario in which he wasn't satisfied with life for another. He even rang Judith to moan about his broken nights with the new baby.

Recently Judith went into her local café, and there was Roger. They'd seen each other in the interim, had these phone calls, but there was a sense of potential territorial conflict. I'm very attached to my café; I think if Peter and I split up I'd ask them to ban him.

'Was he already there? Did you sit at the same table or did he sit at yours?'

I like to know these details. She doesn't expand, however.

'I ordered a piece of chocolate cake and he said he didn't want anything. Then when mine came, he started eating it. It was strangely intimate.'

I'll tell you one thing, mate: you might think you can get away with leaving me, but you're not having my bloody cake — or eating it. Just the thought of it makes me quite annoyed.

And just when it sounds as though she had come to terms with the disaster, and was starting to rise above it:

'He told me they were getting married. I'd just been out shopping and got some sensible work shoes. And after I got this news, I went back and changed them for a pair of high-heels — which I've never worn. The day of the wedding, I went to the seaside with my brother and sobbed all over him.'

Yet this story does have a happy ending.

'I knew I wanted to be with someone, but had no idea how to go about it. A couple of my friends' husbands came round — on their own — and said things like, 'You know I've always been fond of you, Jude: how about a drink sometime?''

She looks somewhat shocked at this: so am I. In fact, I'm horrified. There I was, wondering if she'd had fewer invitations after Roger left, and there were her friends' husbands coming round and practically dropping their trousers in the hall. And bear in mind she's a straightforward, sincere woman — attractive with really nice clothes, but who doesn't wear make-up — and certainly not a big fat flirt like me. So she would never have brought it on herself. Incidentally, if any of my friends are reading this and ever get divorced, please be reassured that I will not be round in fishnets and a miniskirt the minute you've gone.

'Stuart worked at the same hospital [she is an NHS manager]. He was a great person, and I remember thinking, I must invite him round; he and Roger would get on really well. And one day we were sitting in his office, and I said, 'I think my husband's having a mid-life crisis.' And he said, 'Never mind: I've just come back from America with loads of Hershey Bars.' He spread them all out on the desk and it was just wonderful somehow.'

You couldn't win me over with such inferior chocolate. Having said that, she did get the last sane, single forty-something man in London.

'He asked me out for a drink, and though it was just as friends, I felt really good about myself when I was with him. Whereas Roger had been endlessly soul-searching and 'staring into the black hole', Stuart was very at ease with himself and steady, and I was very attracted by that.'

He wore the occasional tank top, and brought green bed sheets when he moved in, but nobody's perfect.

'The week before he moved in, he left armfuls of gladioli on the bonnet of my car. It was lovely, though the car did look like a hearse.'

And here's an odd thing: she doesn't mind the similarities between the two men.

'It's been surprisingly reassuring. For example, the fact that he can eat exactly the same food for lunch every day. Also that he's a very careful driver, and the dark sense of humour.'

It's admirable, even enviable, to reach the point where you can notice that your second husband reminds you in a few ways of your first, and not feel sick at the thought.

'Being married again feels totally different. At twenty, life seemed to stretch for ever, whereas now we both feel we must make the most of our time together. I was always hopeless at relishing the moment: I've got better at that now and that's because of being with Stuart.'

She ends the conversation on a wonderful image which has stayed with me. Every time I think of it I smile.

'The day the Decree Absolute came through the door I was in the kitchen, making coffee. And as usual, the dog snatched the post from the letter box and tried to eat it. I got it away from her and read it, but it still has teeth marks.'

26

Adultery, Desertion, Behaviour
(*Simon*)

So what happens if you do, as a friend of Peter once put it, go to the edge of the cliff and jump off?

I ask Simon, a neighbour who handles divorce cases. Over the course of twenty-five years he reckons he's done about four thousand of them. Four thousand! Imagine — all that pain, all those tears. All those broken hinges on endlessly slammed doors.

Simon doesn't look or sound particularly like my idea of a barrister. He doesn't have a booming voice or a sarcastic manner — 'Come, come now, Miss Stackpole! Do you really expect the jury to believe that you were *not* planning to murder your husband from the very moment he left the top off the toothpaste?'

Nor does he dress as if expecting to be called to run a top city brokerage firm at any moment. He is warm and friendly with tousled hair and glasses that give him a hint of being quick on the uptake, but not precocious, schoolboy. If ever I had to do the dreaded deed, I could possibly stand to do it with him.

In this modern age of instant everything, quickie divorces and websites offering the DIY option, it seems almost anachronistic that most people do still go to court. And because it's a place of strict rules and formality, I find it hard to imagine discussing one's most intimate relationship there. Talking about sex and infidelity is surely bad enough, but your finances! Being married can be a right pain, but the thought of having to go to court, like a criminal, and tell strangers all your stuff, and then quite possibly being humiliated, and paying for it! It seems unimaginable. Yet this is of course what my parents did, and every year about another 130,000 do, too. Peter and I currently know at least four couples who have divorced within the last few years, and in that group three of them are constantly interrupted, and indeed distressed, by having to attend hearings to argue about money and contact with the children — their partners' if not their own, like some hideous tumour you keep having zapped which never goes away.

I ask Simon what brings people to his chambers.

'Well,' he says, 'people have been through a

hell of a lot by the time they get to me. I'm the end of the line, as it were.'

He only handles disputes about money, i.e. no residency or contact orders which are dealt with separately. But does money often represent something else to people?

'Oh yes. When people want a fight, they need something to fight about,' he explains, 'and money is very easy to fight about. Divorce itself is not easy to fight about because it's so easy to obtain.'

'I suppose it is. But people still don't do it lightly.'

'No, but the hurdle has been lowered over the years, and it's now felt that it's stupid to keep unhappy people together. You've got to be a nutter to fight a divorce these days. And/or suffer from a monumental degree of self-righteousness.'

Well, quite. It seems the days are gone when the husband would lean against the fireplace, put his thumbs in his waistcoat and say, 'I refuse irrevocably to release you, Wilhemina.'

Yet there are religious groups which are still vociferously anti-divorce in any circumstances, as if unhappy people deserve to be punished further and releasing themselves from the situation is merely an act of selfishness rather than — as was the case with my parents — saving each other from further pain. It can, many people don't realize, be an act of compassion.

'Are you saying no one contests them any more? Ever?'

'Not really. I've only had one contested in twenty-five years and that one was for purely monetary reasons.'

'That seems extraordinary. What are the grounds these days?'

'You need to have Adultery, Behaviour or be separated for two years if both sides consent. Five years if one of them doesn't consent. Or there's Desertion, which no one ever pleads. Behaviour's the most popular.'

Like what?

'Ooh. It can be almost anything . . . Thirty years ago a judge would have looked for something really eye-catching, like a history of sustained violence. Now you might say, 'He doesn't pay me any attention,' which in the past you'd have been expected to put up with.'

'And that might be enough? I'd have thought *most* wives say their husbands don't pay them enough attention. I mean, if that's grounds — '

'Well, quite possibly. People do come in with some fairly trivial complaints. 'He farts in bed,' that sort of thing.'

Blimey. That's me out.

'So what's the least I could get away with?'

'You could say, for example, 'He won't discuss the things that matter.''

I see a bit of a theme emerging here, of women disgruntled that men don't listen or engage with the emotional issues. Not this again! Are men really still so bad at it?

'Well, the significant majority of petitioners are women.'

'Really? I never knew that.'

In 2006, 41,771 divorces were awarded to husbands and 90,662 to wives. And 129 to both. The 129 were apparently 'cross-petitions', where both bring a case against each other. But what difference does it make who brings it?

'It should make no difference at all who's the divorcer and who the divorcee, as one often finds oneself telling one's client. But it matters an awful lot to some people . . . control, losing face, an inability to accept that one's spouse could have any scintilla of justification to complain about one's behaviour, etc.'

He believes that for quite a lot of people, it's not only justice, fairness and so on that they want.

'It's not so much *what* they're fighting about; it's having the fight. It's a form of catharsis — a very expensive one.'

'Really? I never thought about it like that.'

'It's the fight they should have had when they were together, because they might have got it out of their systems, they might have reached an accord, and so they might have come through it.'

Whooh. So all those arguments I have with Peter might not be so deadly after all. This puts our marriage in an entirely new light.

'It's like throwing up, in the sense that many people desperately avoid it for as long as possible, hoping it will just go away and never have to be confronted and dealt with.'

What a startling yet apposite analogy.

'Then lots of them end up spending a fortune having that fight.'

'How much?'

'Well, the biggest bill I ever saw was for £600,000, a couple in the wholesale garment business, both of whom, it was alleged, were 'parking' money — i.e. hiding it — with third parties, some of whom were offshore companies. And that was just the cost of the money proceedings. But here's the thing. Occasionally it can go all the way to a final hearing, you get a bad result and you come out thinking the client's going to be hopping mad. And they just shrug their shoulders, as though, deep down, they always knew what was likely to happen — as you'd in fact been telling them . . . '

'They *do*?'

'Yes. They're not devastated by not getting the outcome they were struggling to achieve. They just wanted to have the fight.'

'It seems a terrible waste of money. I mean, it'd be cheaper to stay at home and yell at each other for free.'

'Quite — as I constantly tell them!'

But when is arguing constructive, useful and air-clearing, and when merely corrosive?

'A lot of relationships break down due to lack of communication.'

And that, surely, is the crux of the whole thing. Not to blame men all the time, I'd like to point out that women aren't *always* the ones who Talk About Things. Far from it. I think they often imagine men should telepathically know what they want. I feel I've spent quite a lot of my life listening to the various grievances of girlfriends who wouldn't come out with it to the one person who actually needed to hear it: the man. I tell Simon about a cartoon my dad once did, of a man saying, 'What do you want in life?' And the woman's replying, 'I want you to know without my telling you.'

'Hah!' he says. 'So true.'

I also tell him about a friend of ours whose

203

wife moaned to all their friends for years. But he never seemed to be aware of the problem, and they never seemed to talk properly about whatever was bothering her. She was just negative about pretty much everything: his job, her job, where they lived, and so on. Then finally he left her for someone else. And she was absolutely flabbergasted: totally horrified and amazed. Simon nods, unsurprised.

'I asked another family lawyer for some tips on staying married and the one that really stuck in my head was 'Say what you feel.''

'Oh, absolutely!' he says. 'Dead right.'

I may be a woman but I actually learned how to talk about things from Peter, who is, after all, a man. I tell Simon:

'Basically, my only form of conflict resolution was leaving. One night, quite early on, we had some kind of disagreement and he stood by the door and said, 'You're not leaving until you talk to me about this.''

He nods again.

But where was I supposed to have learned it from? I grew up with no experience of either compromise or negotiation.

'When my parents hit a rough patch they didn't deal with it, they just slept with other people.'

'Oh!'

He probably wasn't expecting to hear this.

I might even have embarrassed him. But surely, if they'd talked properly, gone for help perhaps, things could have been different. Not that I wish they'd stayed together: I just feel a little sad that they were so unaware of how to find a solution.

'So do you sometimes wonder how anyone manages it?' I ask him.

Amazingly, it seems not. Unlike me, he's not astonished that people can live together in pairs without exploding or erupting or driving each other crazy.

'Most people work hard to manage their marriages,' he says. 'To compromise, to adapt and to make it a way of life that will work and give them pleasure. And it does need work.'

'Are some people just lazy, then?'

'Some are *very* lazy. People are more impatient now, and more intolerant, and have much higher expectations of what life is going to bring them — on a plate.'

'So what should you do? What shouldn't you do? How can I proof my marriage against failure?'

He's done four thousand divorces. He must know something.

'You can't. You've got to have the sensitivity, and the intelligence, to understand what's going to make it gel and what's going to ruin it.'

And with that he gets up and reaches for his bike. And I realize the thing about him that's most surprising: not the crumpled clothes, not the schoolboy hair, not the warm, undominating manner.

It's that he's done four thousand divorces and he's not cynical. He clearly still believes in the fundamental goodness of people. And to be able to take that away from a conversation about the Worst-Case Scenario really is very inspiring. When Peter comes in I tell him all about it, quickly, before an argument can break out.

'You won't believe this,' I say, 'but we're actually doing quite a lot of things right.'

'Blimey.'

And with that extraordinary revelation hanging in the air, I start the evening meal.

27

Me and Meryl Streep in the Bath

After supper one night Peter says there's a film on he wants to watch. Nothing unusual there, except that it's *The Bridges of Madison County*, a definite girls' film, though since he almost always falls asleep about twenty minutes in, it makes little difference. We stopped going to the theatre after he slept through Simon Callow's Dickens, and I can't give up the cinema so just have to put up with it there, but at least sleeping through films at home is free. I wouldn't mind, but sometimes he wakes up — right towards the end — and says,

'Hm! Not much happened in that, did it?'

Bridges is a bit of a girls' film, as I say, but more important, it's a believable and moving portrayal of what happens if you're married — not miserably — and you meet someone else, and become consumed with wanting them. Do you give up everything? By the way, though it is considered the finest example of the 'Will they or won't they?' genre, I don't count *Witness* as presenting the same dilemma, since no one in their right mind is going to give up cars, telephones and flush lavatories — never mind grow a beard without a moustache — even for Kelly McGillis. And you just know that if Harrison did become an Amish, the romance would be dead in about a week, or in less time than it takes to say, 'Pass me the traditionally hand-carved winnowing tool, Jacob.'

'Why d'you want to watch it?' I say.

'I want to know what happens when a relatively contentedly married person is confronted by a passion that appears to be perfect.'

'Why d'you want to know that?'

'No reason', he says. 'Just curious.'

I tell him,

'It is a women's film, you know.'

I saw it when it came out. I remember smouldering looks across one of those really small fifties kitchen tables, and Clint Eastwood and Meryl Streep in the bath. It ranks alongside *The English Patient* and *Body Heat* as one of the three best films of the last thirty years in which people consumed by an impossible passion share a bath. Actually, come to think of it, more than thirty years ago people in films didn't have baths together. And fifty years ago they didn't even have sex; they just leaned back until the screen went blurred. And seventy years ago, they didn't even do that; they just kissed and volleyed wisecracks back and forth. That was my favourite time.

As it happens, Peter and I had a bath together not that long ago; he sat behind me and I leaned back languidly and squashed his balls.

'Kathleen Turner wouldn't have done that,' he said. 'Nor Kristin Scott-Thomas.'

But he forgave me, because marriage is about give and take.

Kathleen Turner and Kristin Scott-Thomas are not only the two actresses in the other two great bathing films, they're also the two he finds most irresistible. And now we are going to watch Meryl Streep, another of his all-time favourites, so he will have seen all three of his ideal women in the bath. All four, if you include me.

'When you say a 'women's film' . . . ' he says.

'I mean they fall in love and look at each other a lot, and no one gets shot or has a car chase.'

'So what's it about?'

'You said it yourself. You're going along, having a relatively happy life — it's not spectactular but it's OK — and suddenly someone bursts into your life — '

'Who represents an unattained passion.'

'Whom you desperately, *desperately* want to have sex with. Of course I can't imagine that,' I say.

'Of course.'

'But on the other hand, this is Clint Eastwood.'

I have a thing for Clint Eastwood, not a George Clooney, have dinner at his house on the lake with sparkling repartee thing, but a dark, smouldering thing, a thing that as he has got older, and despite his being a staunch Republican — is there any other kind? — has not gone away. When I think of him standing brooding in half-silhouette in a doorway in *Unforgiven*, I can easily imagine leaving my husband, although in that particular fantasy I have to do a quick edit as he goes everywhere on horseback and I'm terrified of hooves.

In *Bridges* at least they have wheels. Meryl Streep plays Francesca Johnson, an Italian-born housewife living quietly with her husband and two teenage children in the Midwest. Clint is Robert Kincaid, a photographer for *National Geographic* magazine, driving round in a pickup truck doing a feature on bridges.

'These bridges,' says Peter. 'They're not immediately the most romantic of images. I mean, it's not as though we're talking about, say, the Golden Gate, or the Clifton

Suspension Bridge.'

The Clifton Suspension Bridge, of course, is where we first lived together, in the next street to its eastern end. On summer evenings we used to go out and look at it, all lit up in its monumental splendour like a massive great tiara across the Avon Gorge.

But the bridges in the film are dreadfully mundane: boring flat walkways with ugly red corrugated-iron roofs.

'He's going to have his work cut out falling in love round those.'

Also, Clint is quite a bit older in this than I remembered. He has grey hair that is thinning on top — no hair plugs for him — but is far too thick round the back. He also has not only a rather lined face, with extremely thick eyebrows that, when his eyes close, as they do constantly, descend over his eyelids in a rather Muppetish way, there's a crease down one side of his face, like you get when you accidentally go to sleep on a fold of sheet.

I nip to the Mac and look up imdb.com.[1]

'My God,' I say. 'When he made this film he was sixty-five.'

'I've got another few years then,' says Peter.

'To do what?'

---

[1] The Internet Move Database.

'Never mind.'

Meryl Streep is forty-five, but playing about thirty-five.

'She has quite substantial calves,' I say.

'She is — irresistible,' he sighs.

He's right. She's so gorgeous I almost fancy her too.

'Can you see yourself as the photographer, driving round?' I say.

'God, yes. I've always thought Clint and I have a lot in common.'

'Er, such as . . . ?'

'The ability to be sensitive and yet, when the situation calls for it, brutal.'

'Except in his case it means making love to beautiful women and shooting baddies, not crying at the end of The Railway Children and shouting at squirrels.'

Clint has taken Meryl round some bridges and come back to her farmhouse for dinner. Her husband and children are conveniently away for four days at the Illinois State Fair.

'The silver apples of the moon, the golden apples of the sun,' he says casually as they take the night air — not a line most people would immediately associate with the man who stood behind a .44 Magnum and said, 'Ask yourself, 'Do I feel lucky?' Well, do ya, punk?'

'Ah, W.B. Yeats,' says Meryl, whose

character used to be a teacher.

'You don't go around quoting Yeats,' I say.

'Instead of reading car magazines?' he says. 'Come on. You'd hate it.'

He's right. The thing is, Clint Eastwood can spout poetry that would make anyone else sound like a complete tosser and still make you want to shag him. He is wearing red braces, mind you. And sixty-five . . . Hmm.

Meryl is better dressed. She's wearing a fifties off-the-shoulder dress with sparkles in it and a full skirt. I am wearing a fifteen-year-old nightie, a black cardigan from Gap and bright pink, extra thick socks. And my legs are overdue for a shave.

Clint is spellbound. He and Meryl, or probably their body doubles, have sex in a very dim light. You can't make out anything much except for a lot of shoulders.

'He's got really weird hair on his back,' says Peter.

'That's her, you fool; she's on top, for God's sake.'

I wouldn't mind a body double — not for sex, which I don't have often enough to want to delegate — but for things like parents' evenings and the dentist.

Now they're in the bath.

'Great tits,' we both say at once.

It's full-frame, so you can see they're hers.

She's lying against him on her back, so neither of them has to have the tap end, though come to think of it, I can't see any taps. You have to use that position if you have a bath in a film, otherwise if they face each other you get huge amounts of knees.

'I can't see any taps, can you? Maybe the props man has removed them.'

'We used to talk about the Tap End of Life,' he says, ruminatively. 'Do you remember?'

'Did we? No I don't.'

'Er, it might have been another girlfriend.'

I like it when he says 'another girlfriend', as if we haven't known each other so long that if we stopped to think about it, we'd be completely freaked out. I mean, we have both been sleeping with the same, one person now for *twenty years*.

Clint asks Meryl to run away with him and after much agonised deliberation she says no. Her husband and children come back, having won first prize for their bull at the fair, but you can see, as she gazes longingly up the road, that her mind is on Other Things. The last time she sees him is at the traffic lights in town. His pickup is in front of theirs and for a long time after the lights change he doesn't pull away. Meryl knows he is waiting for her in case she wants to leap out and come with him. Her hand is on the door handle, then

214

— gasp! The husband hoots the horn and Clint drives away.

'Very good,' says Peter. 'Very believable.'

And I say,

'What if she'd leapt out and run towards the pickup, and *then* the lights changed? He might not have seen her because of the rain, and if he wasn't looking in his mirror . . . Oh my God, and then he would have driven away and she would have been left standing there, her husband knowing she wanted to leave, but — ohhh, the humiliation!'

'Yes,' says Peter. 'But not in Hollywood.'

'Or what if — what if she ran up and did get into the pickup and he pulled away too suddenly and stalled?!'

He pauses, wine glass, wine bottle and my empty Maltesers bag in hand, and looks at me. I think it's the 'What kind of person have I married?' look. Yep, it is.

'If that was us, I'd run out and get in the pickup and when it stalled, you'd get out of your truck and offer to help.'

'Christ, you make me sound like a complete wimp!'

'No, you see, because that's when I'd go back to you. Clint'd be sitting there, uselessly pumping the gas, and you'd say, 'You've flooded it, mate,' and I'd realize you were the man for me all along.'

215

'So I have my uses.'

There's also a fifth possible scenario.

'Knowing my luck, the two of you would get into a conversation about damp distributor heads and he'd forget all about me and go off for a drink with you, leaving me in the rain.'

'Well, that'd be his loss.'

'And what about you?'

'I could never leave you.'

'Even with my constant interrupting and spiky legs?'

'I'll always love you, you know that. Even if you are impossible.'

He puts his arms round me and squeezes me, and we go into the hall, to be assailed by the usual gust of cold air from the great big gap under the front door.

'It's freezing *and* the heating's gone off again. I thought you were going to reset the timer.'

'I did.'

We get into bed and snuggle together like spoons. My feet are cold, so I put them against his legs.

'Jesus. Clint Eastwood wouldn't let you do that.'

'You don't know. He might like it.'

'He may look tough, but only I can withstand the shock of your freezing feet.'

'Hey, I'm too awake. Will you bore me to sleep?'

Clint Eastwood has made over fifty films and can get away with quoting Yeats in red braces, but only Peter can lull me to sleep with highlights from the industrial disputes of the British motor industry.

'Don't make it too interesting though.' On several occasions when he's done this, I've ended up sitting with my head against his chest, begging to hear more. You wouldn't think the Decline and Fall of British Leyland could be that gripping, but that's his secret weapon. Mind you, another time, when he read me one of his short stories, I went off almost immediately.

'OK, how about the Purchase of Jaguar by Ford?'

'Yeah. But remember: not too interesting.'

'I know I am completely fascinating,' he says. 'But I'll try.'

28

How the Unicorn Regained Its Horn

Imagining Peter restarting Clint's pickup truck reminds me once more how strange and unpredictable it is, how we end up loving the people we do. I'd have expected to marry a man who can make me laugh *and* is talented and kind and a wonderful father, even if he is irritating in a hundred different ways. But I could never have dreamed of loving someone so practical. When the oil runs out and it all floods and goes haywire, he'll be able to fashion us a crude shelter from bubble wrap and tell the children a story while he does it.

And what will I be doing? Watching in awe. In the world in which I grew up, Practical Man was heard of but never sighted, as mythical a creature as a centaur. My dad couldn't do anything with nails, a hammer or even a screwdriver. He had no handiness skills whatsoever. And my mother inhabited a very female world, mostly of mothers who were also on their own. Her boyfriends did not so much as change a tyre or even put up a picture. The only one who did any DIY was a gay friend of hers who built a pergola for our climbing roses, and he had transgender surgery shortly afterwards and became a woman.

So you can see how Peter would have seemed exotic.

This is not merely a man who built the children a summer house from a truckload of timber and a sheaf of incomprehensible plans. He takes on a problem, or a situation, and devotes his entire being to solving it. Something which was previously broken becomes fixed. A door that didn't close properly now does. Or a chest that used to lean forward, causing its drawers to slide open as if propelled by poltergeists, has tiny wedges attached to its feet to render it stable. It's like a kind of magic. It *is* magic.

And when his solution doesn't work the first time, or goes wrong, he grabs it by the throat and, long after a normal person would have given up, doggedly wrestles it into submission. Sometimes the amount of time and energy expended is disproportionate, but he can't stop. His focus takes on an artistic, almost messianic quality that makes you realize you're in the presence of, if not greatness, then an ability to focus of almost autistic proportions.

A while back the lever inside our cistern broke, rendering the handle all floppy and the lavatory unflushable. When I came upon him, he was:

'In the process of designing a solution.'

'At the moment,' I observed, 'it has a piece of string on it . . . '

'And I'm planning to repair the lever.'

'Wouldn't it just be easier to order the part?'

'Ah, no, you see, because you can't buy just the lever. You have to get the whole unit — for £7!'

Hmm, £7. This is where some wives might have got a little impatient, seeing how much less £7 is than the call-out charge for a plumber. But I was fascinated.

'So I'm doing it with a bit of a plastic milk carton and some glue.'

Now let's be clear about this. This milk carton and glue scenario was no pastiche of a *Blue Peter* project, no botch liable to fall apart at the first flush. This was more in the league of a feat of engineering combined with an art installation. It's still going strong. And so, partly because of it, am I.

I just can't tear myself away.

A couple of years ago, during a very hot summer, he found a new object for his passion. Having moaned at me for years about tottering towers of hummus pots, newspapers in bags and communities of flattened cardboard boxes, he decided, singlehandedly, to reduce the world's landfill mass. Every non-perishable item was either put in the correct container provided by the council, or repurposed in some other way. Some boxes became My Little Pony stables. Others were given to his friend James, for using to pack up the model cars he was selling on eBay. As a result, I soon became conversant with which box fitted which size of car, for example: single soap = one Dinky; toothpaste = two Matchbox Cars, and so on.

'Look at our bin!' Peter said admiringly. 'It's filling up so slowly, we haven't had to put it out for ages!'

'Yes, I know: I can smell it.'

There was more.

'We're going to have compost!' he announced, eyes aflame with the convert's zeal.

As Head Gardener, I was in favour. All our meat-free waste was now emptied into a beehive-shaped wooden box in the garden, and for the first time in eight years the children became fascinated by fruit and vegetables, albeit in their final stages of decomposition.

'Hey, Mum! It's really disgusting in there! Come and see!'

They'd fling open the lid to show their friends, who had innocently come to tea and peered in, half fascinated, half shaken, to witness the unfeasible number of flies. Who needs CGI when you can create something really horrendous in your own home?

Then he graduated to an even more ambitious and supposedly planet-saving, yet almost entirely pointless, project.

Unable to sleep in the heat, I got up one morning about five, and allowed myself a bath, the first in weeks.

'Don't let the water out!' he cried, popping his head round the door.

'Ooh. Are you going to join me?'

No: he had something far more exciting in mind. He leapt downstairs and sprang back into the room with the garden hose.

'We can use this to water the garden. I just have to remember what my father did.'

Thanks to the miracle of DNA I was now able to watch the son of L.S. Grimsdale (Capt, Dec'd) manfully lowering a huge hose into a bath of cold water, in order to siphon it out into the garden. Being full of air it didn't want to stay under, so I had to hold it down. We also had to take down the curtains to protect them from the filthy hose now snaking out of the first-floor window.

'That end needs to be kept on the bottom,'

he explained. 'We coil it up, with no kinks, obviously. Then it will fill up with water all the way along, which will eventually come out the other end.'

'I thought you were supposed to suck it to get it flowing.'

I remembered this from when my mother had her petrol stolen.

'Not when it's 60 feet long.'

'Right.'

After two attempts I suggested we give up and go downstairs for eggs and coffee, but then I'm the daughter of people whose idea of manual labour was lifting a large sheet of card.

At six-thirty Lawrence came in and reacted really quite calmly to the sight of his parents — one naked — apparently subduing a snake in the bath.

'Hi, Mum. Hi, Dad.'

Then we were joined by Lydia.

'What are you doing?! Can I watch?'

'Of course. Here, hold this down.'

She took over, and I was able to stand up and straighten my back. On the third go, we did it. The garden was watered, and there was enough left over to fill the spare wheelie bin, the nearest thing we had to a water butt.

But being a wheelie bin it, of course, had no tap, so the only way we could get any of the water out was by leaning over the side with a watering can. By this method we were able to collect about 5 per cent of it. The remainder very quickly began to smell and due to the bin being too heavy to move, was tipped out near the house, making the patio and most of the garden temporarily uninhabitable.

But thanks to Peter's forensic determination, the garden was watered and one single bath of water saved for the nation. Even with my pathetically impractical background, I could appreciate the satisfaction to be gained from this achievement. I could never have imagined, however, the lengths to which he would go to solve this next problem, which arose that same summer, and which explains — in as far as anything can explain — why we are still married.

School broke up, and we joined Lydia's friends Ella and Louisa and their parents for a week on the Isle of Wight. We went to Compton Beach and rode the waves on body boards — well, the children did; I sat on a sticky blanket and read Redmond O'Hanlon's *Trawler*, definitely the funniest book ever written about gutting halibut in a Force Twelve gale. And we went to the old-fashioned amusement park there, the strangely named Blackgang Chine, where Lydia bought a unicorn.

What, another? I hear you say. For my daughter already had a whole herd. Ah, but:

'This is a special unicorn, Mummy. Look, it's white.'

'Right . . . '

'And it's standing on a beautiful piece of grass with flowers on it.'

'Hmm . . . '

'It's only £1.99!'

That settled it. Lulled homewards by ferry on the shockingly pricey swell of the Solent — about £5 a wave — we were about to disembark when I realized the unicorn was out of its box. It was small, and highly breakable, the sort of toy that should have a warning on the box that says, *Not To Be Played With Other Than in Strictly Controlled Conditions and Certainly Not While Getting Off a Ferry.*

'Lydia, be careful with that,' I said. We're getting off in a minute.'

'I *am*!'

She flew into a sulk, and flounced past me, knocking the unicorn against the edge of the table and snapping off its tiny horn.

'Don't look at me! And don't SAY ANYTHING!'

It was clearly my fault. I felt simultaneously angry and guilty, and she was not even mollified when she found the horn on the vehemently patterned carpet and managed to get it back into the box.

On the way back to London we visited our friends David and Angela in Dorset, who took us to the summer fête at their local hospice, where there were lots of really good plants and books to buy. But because we'd been away for two weeks, the car was full of interesting pebbles and dirty washing. So we could only bring back two plants, two cakes and five books. Plus I had to get some jam. Then we edged slowly into the other jam, the traffic jam that is Dorchester, and started for home. And Lydia dropped the unicorn's horn in the car. The very very full car. The horn which was, at most, 8mm long.

And she wouldn't be placated, but sat for the rest of the journey with her arms folded staring sullenly out of the window.

Back home, we unloaded the cakes and the books, and the gritty beach towels and the sandwich crusts and the interesting pebbles. And Peter excavated the next layer: the comics and Portsmouth Harbour key-rings from the previous year, and apple cores from the last time they ate an apple, so long, long before that. Then he crawled into each footwell. And finally he unscrewed the entire back seat, beneath which he found the horn.

He put it in a small glass on the kitchen

windowsill above the sink, but forgot to tell me this. So later I picked up the glass, tipped it upside down to see if it was empty and clean — it seemed to be — and put it back in the cupboard.

'Right,' he told Lydia later that day. 'I'm going to glue your unicorn's horn back on.'

'Oh, thank you, Daddy! I love you so much!'

'*Where is the glass?*'

This would be the moment, I thought, when my daughter stopped loving me, when her mother, her so-called champion and protector, chucked her unicorn horn down the sink. But I did privately begin to suspect that the unicorn was a Darwinian, and trying to evolve it away. As for what my husband thought of me, he did not say. He merely knelt down and went into Firefighter Mode.

'Right! Move aside.'

Kneeling on the floor, he cleared all the bleach, oven spray, car wax and ancient, stiff cloths out from under the sink, and dismantled the U-bend.

And found the horn.

But he was prevented from glueing it on at that moment because the phone rang. So he put it back in the glass, and the next day while washing up I swung a pan on to the draining board and broke the glass.

And still the horn miraculously remained on the draining board, so I put it in another glass and Peter came back in and glued it on and Lydia loved me again — though, understandably, she loved him more.

And the unicorn stood on the windowsill. *We have such bad luck*, it seemed to be saying. *You can see why we died out.* As for Lydia, she hugged her father gratefully then ran off to watch TV.

And I said:

'I am glad I married you after all.'

And he put on the kettle, and got out two cups, and said:

'You should be.'

29

The Single Strawberry

One Friday night a couple of years back, I strolled into the sitting room, leaned innocently against the sofa and locked my bad knee. I was in pain and couldn't move. Any attempt to edge out of the room or even to sink pathetically on to the sofa made the pain worse. I was stuck, half turned towards the TV and half to the door, like a petrified fleeing figure in Pompeii.

I called:

'Pe-terrrr . . . '

And he came in with the response familiar to any spouse of seventeen years' standing when confronted by their opposite number immobilized by pain.

'Well, just sit down and it'll probably go away.'

That's his answer to everything: the traffic in our road, global warming, the credit crunch: just sit down and it'll go away.

He'd be great at the Ministry of Defence.

'General! They're hacking each other to bits down here. Send troops, quick!'

'Well, just sit down and they'll probably go away.'

Actually, I think for countries that don't have oil or American defence bases, that is their policy.

'I *can't* sit down, you idiot,' I said. 'I can't bloody *move*.'

'Well, sorry! I'm only trying to help.'

What really got me above all was that line.

A female would have been far more sympathetic. Well, most females. Lydia not only had no sympathy but actually told me off for blocking her view of the telly.

Women like to take on the sufferings of others. Men who do that generally have to become messiahs; women just do it as they go about their daily business. Some of our worst arguments have been about people neither of us has ever met, because like most females, I worry deeply about those suffering across the planet in myriad awful ways. Recently my sister asked if I had any clothes for some refugees in her area, and I found I had quite a lot, which I put in one or two carrier bags in the hall.[1] Along came Peter.

'What's all this stuff doing in the hall?'

'That's for the refugee centre. Claire's

---

[1] OK, maybe more than one or two. Definitely no more than three.

friend's collecting stuff. There are these poor women sleeping there, from Cameroon and Darfur. They've been through the most terrible experiences. They've had to flee with their children — some have even lost their children. It's just so horrendous. And they just escape in the clothes they stand up in. So she's been taking them tights and shoes and stuff — even pants. Because you've got to think, they're here in this cold, rainy climate. And they're sleeping on church floors, some of them. They have nowhere to go. It's so awful. I just want to cry when I think about it.'

'Right. So, is it going to be here long? Because I thought we agreed we were going to keep this area clear.'

Note the use of 'I thought we agreed', as if it's the Kyoto Protocol as opposed to some bags in our hall.

It's not that men don't care, or even that women care too much. No, that's exactly what it is. They can see children blown up by car bombs on the news and switch off afterwards, while we worry about the woman in front of us in the supermarket queue whose child's lost a shoe.

The other day we were driving along and saw someone else get flashed by a speed camera. And immediately I switched my attention, not just to the person who got flashed, but to their spouse, imagining them coming in and confessing, if it was a man, and his wife being really angry and upset. Maybe she'd been about to spend that £60 on shoes for the children and now she couldn't. Maybe they had an argument and she went off to her mother's. Maybe he's been reckless with money all through the marriage and this was the last straw. Maybe — OK, I'm stopping now.

Some of us even have such extreme empathy it extends to objects. Lydia may not have cared about my sore knee, but she's been known to feel sorry for a single strawberry in a bowl. And while I pretend to tease her about it when Peter and Lawrence are around, I know how she feels. Forty years on, I can still remember the stab of grief I felt when Danny, a boy in my primary school class, threw the apple I'd given him into the road. It wasn't a romantic overture or anything; he asked for the apple, and I saw a way out of having to eat the fruit my mother had yet again put in my satchel instead of a Penguin. There was just something so tragic in the way it rolled down the road.

This over-empathizing is, I think, also why, when we're upset or sad or vulnerable or pregnant or periodic or just feeling like failures, we expect our men to know immediately how we feel, and to act accordingly — with tea/massage/chocolate/ not that chocolate the other chocolate: you know I don't like that chocolate, and moral support. And why we're always surprised and annoyed if they don't. And, while we're on this point — just to avoid any confusion, the two things we're *not* looking for when we're feeling sad, vulnerable, pregnant, periodic or like failures are:

A pep talk that, however you dress it up, essentially boils down to 'Pull yourself together,' or:

Sex.

The 'Pull yourself together'/'Chin up, chaps!' approach to life is one that my father, who was comfortably in touch with his feminine side, associated with a very specific kind of male, a kind to which he emphatically did not want to belong. This evidently began with his time in National Service, where the sergeant major really did shout at the men in that strange, kind of fragmented vernacular, and referred to my father as 'You with the 'orrible tache!' which roughly translates as: 'You, with the deliberate hair on your upper lip which is also dark, therefore marking you out as not only different but also almost certainly foreign'.

And then, in later life, Dad rather sweetly, though a bit stupidly, believed he could recognize and thus avoid the same type by observing certain key indicators, for example slicked-back hair, BMW ownership, excessive heartiness in the face of bad news — such as rain, strikes, mass unemployment, and a tendency to vote Tory. All these things he linked to a lack of sensitivity towards the feelings of others, a characteristic which was held by almost everyone except him — at least back then — to be the preserve of women.

Incidentally, my friend Richard, of whom I am very fond, is not one of those types, but is prone to displays of chin-upness in the face of other people's — i.e. my — emotional issues, so much so that I've once or twice had to really snap at him, just to get him to see how emotionally vulnerable I was. It's never put him off, though, and even when I once said, 'You're so unfeeling — if you had a problem page you'd call it 'Pull Yourself Together'' He said, quite genuinely, 'Jolly good idea.'

I don't like to generalize about either gender, though being married to Mr Perfect, I sometimes forget what so many women have to put up with. And one of the complaints women make again and again is of men regarding anything 'emotional', e.g. needing TLC while feeling feeble, periodic or pregnant, as being somehow of less value or even not registering at all.

I've had I don't know how many relationships where that element was completely missing. You'd go a bit sad or whatever, and they'd just stand there. Even one of Peter's more viable predecessors, a fundamentally very decent bloke, had no idea. I was depressed. I was in therapy. But I had to get to the brink of utter despair before he came round and said:

'You're feeling a bit down, aren't you?'

I had the paracetamols lined up on the bedside table at the time, so yes.

It's as if the emotional stuff is on a frequency they can't hear, like the communications of bats.

Men of course think women are oversensitive — and they're right. It's why so many American sitcoms used to end with the woman rolling her eyes and the man shrugging, 'What'd I say?'

Des — the one with the mirrored cupboards — once explained to me that men don't know what to do with a crying woman because they tend to prefer concrete problems they can fix. And I was really grateful for this insight.

'Mind you,' he admitted, 'most of us can't fix things either.'

I've heard it said that men can't get involved with feelings because they evolved to put up shelters and kill mammoths, which is just — oh, wait. It wasn't put around by *male* anthropologists, was it? And in any case, that whole evolution theory doesn't account for lots of things; if they needed to see really well to hunt, how come they can't find anything in a cupboard?

A survey I saw recently examined the way in which the sexes perceive themselves by looking at jobs in the home, which were divided into 'Pink' jobs generally undertaken by women and 'Blue' ones supposedly done by men. But what it revealed was not so much what people actually do, as what each sex thinks the other *should* do. For example, Cleaning the Oven was shown as a Pink job because it's mostly done by women, but I think in a lot of homes no one does it. Well, they don't in ours. We have a 'self-cleaning' oven, which means the dirt falls past the sides and collects in a thick, impenetrable layer at the bottom.

And Mending Broken Toys was listed as a Blue job, but nowadays who does that either? You keep them in a cupboard until the child grows out of them then sneak them into the box for the school fête. Then there was Cleaning the Lavatory, a Pink job only because women always get stuck with it, so it's self-perpetuating.

'You've got to clean it. I can't because it's a Pink job, see? Says so right there.'

'Oh, OK. Well, let's see . . . oh yes, Touching Your Willy I see is a Blue job, so . . . night night!'

And that, children, is why surveys are *bad*.

But, look, don't take my word for it. For a really deep insight into this divide, see the episode of *Family Guy* where Peter Griffin is sent to a gender awareness retreat after sexually harassing a woman at work, and it works so well he turns female: starts having long baths with candles and ringing his friends to chat about nothing, which totally freaks them out. I watched it with Lawrence and felt I had to keep saying, defensively:

'But not all women are really like that,' followed immediately by:

'Actually, yes, we sort of are.'

30

He likes a Cuddle After Sex and I Don't (*Maggie and Andre*)

Maggie came into my life through my website Bad Mothers Club. She emailed me one day, and made me laugh.

She was very articulate, with this very composed demeanour, nice clothes and beautiful manners, but at the same time incredibly funny and rude. One of the things she said to me when we first met was:

'You've got very good tits. I mean that Not in a Lesbian Way.'

And NIALW became our favourite sign-off to each other.

The other thing I noticed was her ruthless honesty about her husband Andre, with whom she is frequently frustrated.

I've met him and couldn't see anything wrong with him, but that's marriage, isn't it — a peculiar cocktail of chemicals that react differently when mixed with other elements; your spouse is infuriating mostly, and often only, to you. And each day you help create the conditions to make him so. If Peter's faults were obvious to the world I wouldn't be writing this book. And if he were married to someone else he would be different; still annoying, of course, but differently so.

The question is, how much of it is really his 'fault'? And do we tend to choose people who are going to disappoint us in precisely the ways that we expect to be disappointed? I'm frequently angered by Peter's refusal to deal with potential disagreements, at school, with the council and any situations I see as unjust. And he behaves, on the surface of it, exactly like my mother, who never took my side. Having made sure I didn't marry my father — i.e. someone with a bad temper — I was pretty shattered, as you may imagine, when I realised I'd married my mother. Peter, of course, thinks it's hilarious.

So I'm wondering if Maggie is in a similar pattern. I know from our previous conversations she's not in favour of unnecessary suffering during childbirth, a point on which we agree vehemently. So I'm not surprised when, over lunch one day, she illustrates Andre's own dismissiveness with this example:

'After Sam was born, he said, 'That wasn't so bad!''

She glowers at me.

'It was forty-eight hours: forty-eight hours of pushing out a sofa sideways. I had broken blood vessels all over my face and neck from pushing. Then I was wheeled by a hospital orderly with a Maureen-from-Driving-School sense of direction into one of those grim, green-lit NHS bathrooms that make you resemble a drowned corpse. I stared at my broken-vesselled, drippy-stomached, bleeding self and sobbed: 'I look like the Creature From the Black Lagoon!' It was then he said, 'It wasn't that bad' as though I'd just had a splinter removed.'

Ah yes, and I remember the friend whose husband said, 'We're not having pain relief.' My stomach still tightens when I think about it. There's an upside to everything, as Peter would say.

'He's very organized,' Maggie goes on.

'I'm sorry,' I say, 'but Being Organized is not bad.'

'I know: there's a good side. When we went on holiday to Malaysia he brought a medical bag. It was huge. When he picked it up he dislocated his shoulder. It even had dental tools to do an emergency filling.'

'What, really?'

'Really. But! After three days I got the runs and he went to the bag, and without saying anything, opened it and took out a packet of Immodium. And he followed that up with rehydration salts. Didn't crow at all.'

'That is bloody impressive. When the children hurt themselves or he has a headache, Peter wanders around saying, 'Which one's the paracetamol again?' I can't stand it.'

'He remembers the times and dates of every petty transgression. Like when I 'stole' his pen. He's got times and dates! 'On 14 March 1997 did you or did you not filch my only biro? And replace it with the green ink one that makes me look like a crazed weirdo?' I wouldn't be surprised if he's got CCTV footage of me furtively removing the one pen in our house that works. I feel as though he's got a list of my 'sins' and one day it'll all come out.'

Maggie was brought up a Catholic. Mind you, even though I don't believe in any of that stuff, I do recognize the infuriating way that some people turn themselves into barristers when they're arguing with you. Peter's speciality is to inquire, with a sort of sceptical sneer, 'When did I do that? If you can't tell me when it was . . . ' thus invalidating my entire claim. Who does he think he is, the bloody insurance company? It really does make me want to throw something at him.

'He picks his nose in the shower.'

'Urgh . . . '

'And for ages it would stick on the tiles

241

— calcify like old cereal. I had to practically sandblast it off.'

'*Urgh!*'

Thank God the food hasn't come yet.

'And this really annoyed me, so eventually I cleaned it off with his toothbrush.'

'You didn't.'

Oh my God.

'He found it and I confessed. I did buy him another toothbrush. But he still thought it wasn't a big deal so I pointed out that if he had a new girlfriend there was no way he'd be flicking his bogies about in the shower, was there? But then he added that if I had a new boyfriend I wouldn't fart so loudly either.'

Hm. We're at our usual branch of Carluccio's, and I have to put her on pause while I pour water into my coffee which I always do because they make it so strong. If we were married she'd probably say, 'Just order it weaker, then!' but we're not, so we're incredibly nice to each other.

'If he comes in and doesn't like what I'm watching on television, he sits down and emits waves of silent disapproval.'

'That's a bit — no, very annoying.'

'Then, when I finally switch off *Top Ten Celebrity Shags* or whatever, he silently gets up and puts on what he likes: *When Buildings Fall Down* or *When Trains Attack*.'

'Hah!'

'If he wants to watch a programme, he wants *me* to want to watch it as well.'

'Why?'

'So I can end up saying, 'Hey, you were right! This show *Mega Structures* is really good!''

This makes me think of the American comic Sarah Haskins, and her video piece about the bizarre frequency of ads in which women advise each other to improve their lives by eating yogurt.

Maggie's next problem is a really unusual one. I have never before met a woman who had this complaint to make about a man.

'He's always asking me what I'm thinking: he says he can't 'read' me.'

What wouldn't the female population of the world give to have a man like that!

'He sounds like a girl,' I say.

'I know! I wish he'd leave me alone. It's like he wants to climb into my head. He would no doubt say that I don't open up to him. I just sometimes need to *retreat*, you know?'

'What, into your cave? You really do sound like a bloke.'

'And it's got worse. We had a huge row because he's not interested in my sketching. He never has been. And it's not as though I keep it a big secret from him either. I showed him one of my drawings and said, 'Tell me what you think.' And he liked it, but he had to sort of say something profound that would make me go: 'Oh yes! Why, I've never thought of it that way before!' When I just want him to acknowledge it, not say anything meaningful. He was only trying to help, but . . . '

I think what she's talking about is the underlying assumption that she *needs* any help. Maybe he's a bit alarmed by her talent because it makes him feel spare and unnecessary, in other words redundant. I was talking to a couple the other day, and the bloke had written a song — it wasn't bad, either — and the woman was incredibly dismissive in a sort of 'You know you'll never get anywhere with it, it's pointless' kind of way. And I was horrified because Peter knows his job is to say nice things; offer constructive criticism, sure, but only if it's good.

I think men, far more than women, like to be the Expert. Like the guy I got stuck with once at a salsa class who was really clumsy, and kept giving me advice on how to dance better while he stood on my feet, and totally messed up all the moves. Mind you, my sister once knew a girl who was an Expert on Everything. She would sit there and, with a straight face, explain your own job to you.

Maggie then tells me that the first time she got some interest from a gallery, Andre was surprised.

'I think he's a teensy bit threatened,' I say. 'You might become a big success and leave him behind. You might run off with your art dealer.'

'I used to be far more reliant on him,' she says. 'I left him for a while. I had PND and was in a bad way for about eight months.'

'Hang on: you left him?'

'Yes.'

'And came back?'

This was after Sam was born.

'But that's when I started to draw.'

This brings us to the Iceberg Theory, which I've concluded is at the root of a great deal of people's dissatisfaction with each other.

This is The Iceberg Theory:

Quite a few years before I met Peter, when I was still ricocheting between men who were unavailable, sexy-but-mean or slightly dull, I met someone I really liked. He was very unselfish in bed — unlike far too many of them who'd peer at me blankly after sex as if I was some remote-controlled toy which had failed to work. I blame the cinema: all those women throwing their heads back and gasping when the man's done nothing at all. And we got on well. There was just one

245

problem: I was a writer and he didn't read. So we couldn't talk about books or any of that, because he wasn't interested. Whenever I talked about it, he'd get this pained look on his face. So I just stopped, so as not to make him feel uncomfortable. But it meant avoiding something quite big, a major detour. Then I began to realize that hiding such an important part of myself was never not going to be a problem, because the more I suppressed it, the more it wanted to burst out — like a pregnancy under a school pinafore. And if he didn't like that part of me we couldn't possibly be together in the end. I put it off and put it off but eventually I couldn't stand it any more and I broke up with him. And that's the Iceberg Theory: the more you ignore it and keep sailing, the more likely it is to rip a bloody great hole in the marriage and sink it.

But I don't say this to Maggie, even when she says, 'He says that he's 'developed and matured' during the marriage whereas I've 'changed'.'

She gestures two lines diverging.

'Maybe you've become more confident,' I say.

Then the food arrives, and I eat too quickly, partly because I'm hungry and partly so I can swap my fork for my pen again and get down what she says. And again, she says something I've never heard from a woman before.

'I never stroll or amble, I march. I have tall parents and when I was small I had to learn to keep up with them. He always wants to stroll — with his arm round me.'

'And that's a Bad Thing?'

She gives a kind of snort.

'We went to Paris for a romantic weekend and I was doing my usual route march. So he put his arm round me and said, 'Let's just *amble* down the Champs-Elysées,' and apparently I snapped, 'I hate ambling!''

She lets me finish her *Milanese di Pollo*, which she would never do if we were married. I ate some chips off Peter's plate recently, and he got really annoyed. It was just that I was hungry and it was quite hard to stop. And because we were watching television I thought he might not notice.

We look at the pudding menu and don't choose one — because we're full, not because we're afraid of getting fat.

'The longer we're together,' she says, 'the more he becomes like a woman and I resemble a man. He's more romantic than me. He does remember my birthday, he does bring me flowers. And every single year I forget our anniversary.'

'You're kidding.'

I don't care about anniversaries but an awful lot of women do.

'Every year we have the same conversation:

'D'you know what day it is today?'

'Oh *bollocks*!''

She looks at me and sighs.

'He likes a cuddle after sex, and I don't. I *must* be a bloke I suppose.'

'Still. You do *have* sex.'

'When he wants to do it, he lies on the bed waggling his legs 'endearingly'.'

'His *legs*?'

'Yep. The first time he did it I thought he was having a stroke.'

Peter sometimes trots naked across the room with a 'keen' expression on his face, but then he's given up trying to seduce me and is now just going for laughs.

When the bill arrives I get out my card, and she says,

'Oh, are you *sure*?'

'Well, there you are,' I say. 'You are a girl after all.'

31

Nocturnal Transactions

Sometimes I listen to Lawrence and his friend Milo talking about the characters in the book they're making together, or Lydia and her friend Daphne repeating their hilarious nonsense routines with the funny little phrases and gestures, and I just pray they don't ever let it go.

It doesn't happen nearly as much nowadays, but when I was young a lot of girls believed that their 'real' life began on their wedding day, and that everything before that was just dead time. From the age of nine, for about a year, I drew my future wedding dress over and over again on my exercise books: silver satin with real diamonds and pearls. Even university graduates were often encouraged to become typists. Why not? Most of them were probably going to get married and give up work anyway.

The other loss after marriage was often of friends. Girlfriends were what you had before you got a husband, like dolls; you went through a door and when you got to the other side you

249

were half of a couple. Peter constantly says I should see more of mine; he understands there's no substitute for the company of females — and I do become PMTish and miserable when I don't.

As for men, they were expected to stop playing with cars and train sets and become responsible family men. And they didn't play with their children nearly as much as they do now, so they couldn't even sneak back into the toy cupboard via their own kids. Airfix planes, model magazines and even precious record collections were evicted to make room for cocktail cabinets, sideboards and the other trappings of wedlock. Before everyone started bashing down the walls of their kitchens, the middle-class thing to have was a dining room, an entirely pointless space given over to a polished table — which, naturally, you couldn't put anything on, and which was used about twice a year. All the fun stuff — LPs, posters, comics — had to be relegated to the garage or attic, if you had one. And if you didn't . . .

Why, when we marry, do we give up our youthful selves? I know my father was immature, but his childishness was also the best thing about him. So why must we 'grow out of' our carefully preserved discs, DVDs, toy cars — and often the old mates that go with them?

Peter and I once had dinner with a couple from school, who were clearly getting on very badly. They didn't look at each other at all during the meal, and barely spoke. We left as soon as we politely could. But before we did, the wife insisted on giving us a tour of the house. It was all very expensively done, and the only thing that got her really animated. Incidentally, I can appreciate a love of interiors; I've been known to get slightly aroused at the sight of a really good bathroom myself. But this was in such an unhappy atmosphere. The last room we came to was quite small, and had a Pink Floyd poster on the wall, a shelf of old singles and a guitar.

'That's John's room,' she said, rolling her eyes.

That said it all. He'd been completely sullen all evening, but we suddenly both felt terribly sorry for him. I like to think that Guitar Hero is already saving marriages all over the world, because yes, Lawrence, as you have frequently told me: computer games are not stupid at all.

It was after that grim evening that Peter and I realized we had two things definitely going for us: we haven't run out of things to

251

say to each other, and we respect each other's toys.

I particularly felt for that poor man because he was a music nerd and I once lived amongst them. I was merely a fan, who loved the music, wrote about it — not very knowledge-ably — and spent my nights on the dance floor. But I also mixed with the ones who really *knew* the music, who never danced, and spent their weekends at record fairs collecting rare vinyl that they took around in crumpled carrier bags. One of them had a Chuck Berry 78[1] that he never let out of his sight.

I wouldn't have slept with any of these guys; as far as I know, no one did. But their knowledge! You had to respect that. There was another, Graham, who worked for a record company and had over 3,000 albums. He did get married, but I heard that his wife made him get rid of them, which I hope, really hope, isn't true. I *know* they wouldn't have had enough space, and I *know* that at some point they probably had children and no normal person can afford an extra bedroom just for LPs. But — I somehow can't bear the idea that he let them go.

---

[1] Long-playing, thick vinyl record that rotated at 78 revolutions per minute and predated the LP (33rpm) and the single (45rpm).

I loved my records, but the treasures of my childhood have the strongest pull. My annuals, *Bunty, Jinty, Misty, Girl, Sally and Diana*, 1958 to 1978, sit on a shelf in the tiny, narrow room where we do the ironing. Every now and then Peter makes noises about having a clearout — only preliminary noises, mind — but when he does, I simply refer him to the shelves above, and the seventies and eighties LPs, forty or so old editions of *Classic Car* magazine, about thirty Thomas the Tank Engine books from the mid-fifties, three huge bound volumes of *Meccano* magazine and two Scalextric sets, including the one I gave him when we got married.[1]

I don't think you should have to lose touch with that bit of yourself: the bit that when you're a child, means you line up your dolls or your cars in a certain order, and become furious if your mother clears them away. So I think when it gets threatened and messed around with, that bit of you, it feels like being quite small again.

Peter thinks it's a question of balance, that

---

[1] He gave me a silver whisky flask with my name inscribed on it, presumably on the assumption that I would be needing a drink on a regular basis.

253

one should not try to involve the spouse beyond Standard Levels of Tolerance.

'I don't tell you about my eBay transactions,' he observes.

'Transactions, as in: things you have bought?'

It sounds like some dreadful euphemism: 'nocturnal transactions'.

'How much are you spending on there then, anyway?'

'See? That's why I don't involve you.'

It makes no difference, as it happens, since in my capacity as Head of Money I'm the only one who reads the bank statements and knows how to do online banking. I could whip all the money away to the Cayman Islands if I wanted — though I'd rather we went to the Cayman Islands and the money stayed here.

'You only lasted four hours at the Goodwood Festival of Speed,' he says, changing tack in a mild admonishment of my supposed impatience with automotive pur-suits — which is a bit rich.

'Er, hang on. Number one, four hours is quite *long* to stand around in a paddock looking at cars. And two, it was a glamorous occasion with champagne. It would have been one hour otherwise.'

I love champagne, and will go — almost

— anywhere to drink it, even to a field in Sussex to have my eardrums blown out by six-litre vehicles revving up a slope.

'Need I remind you that I have a deep appreciation of the Internal Combustion Engine,' I remind him, 'which underpins the marriage.'

'True,' he admits. 'But you would never be one of those women sitting on the picnic chairs, with the thermos flasks.'

He means the ladies with their anoraks zipped right up who accompany their husbands to classic car shows, again in fields, where they sit beside their Rover P4s or MG Midgets, sipping tea and gazing into the distance.

'Of course not,' I say. 'There's never any champagne.'

People should be able to keep their hobbies, but — I'm with Peter on this — in moderation.

'I wouldn't, for example, expect a woman to put up with engines in the front room,' he says, unnecessarily.

'Good God! Do we know anyone like that?'

'Keith Hill. He used to fix my Citroëns.'

The cars that went up and down: I'd forgotten. We went to his house once to collect Peter's DS21, and there were two on the front lawn and two down the side with three more round the back.

'All', says Peter, 'in various states of disrepair.'

'Was he ever married, though?'

'Oh yes. And kids.'

I'm flabbergasted. Maybe the house just became surrounded by more and more cars until she couldn't get out.

32

Marital Satnav

So yes, I love cars more than most females. On the other hand, we've had two of our worst ever arguments in the car. Are you surprised?

No.

While many families we know now have satellite navigation in their cars, we have stuck to our traditional system for finding our way to new places — an A–Z which we can no longer see properly because the print is too small and a row. Satnav is legendary for sending people the wrong way; the newspapers are dotted with stories of frustrated villagers moaning about lorries driving into their fields, and ambulances taking patients 200 miles up the M1 and back down again to the town they started from, all because the satnav told them to. But in its favour, it must have considerably reduced the number of marital fracas that take place in cars — if only because of the introduction of a common enemy.

Some people feel that regional accents

enhance the experience, making it less robotic and more human. But there's another potential application for this technology which has been missed. For those who travel alone and miss the company of the loved one, a simple software tweak would allow the system to be programmed with the voice of their actual spouse, recreating the flavour and intimacy of the relationship.

So instead of the dry, boring instruction 'In 200 metres, turn left,' you would have: 'I said *second* left. Second, as in 'the one after first'?'

And:

'Since when is that the way to my sister's? I mean, how many times have we done this journey? A *million*?!'

Then:

'By the postbox! I said BY THE POST-BOX! The round red thing. Jeez . . . '

Followed by, for Peter specifically:

'How long have you lived in London, you great big Yorkshire twat?'

And so on.

He's got a better idea though: Female Satnav, which he thinks would be hilarious.

'Can you imagine?! It'd be full of useless information, like:

'Turn right by the pub that used to be the Pint and Breathalyser — ooh, what's it called now? Kim had her hen night there . . . '

'And: 'Left! No, no, right! God, I can never remember which is which, can you?'

'And: 'It's just up here, by the bus stop. I don't know which bus stop! How many are there in South Norwood? God . . . ''

Hilarious. Actually my sister once bought a television from a woman who gave her address as 'near the bus stop'. And this was in Ashford, a reasonably sized town, as opposed to, say, a hamlet with one road.

Hilarious indeed, but ever so humungously ironic, because my husband is married to a woman who has an excellent sense of direction and can read maps. Let me amend that: who has an excellent sense of direction, can read maps and *can drive at the same time* — which she frequently *has* to as when it's his turn to do it he *never bothers*. To give you an example:

ME (DRIVING): Which way?

HIM (WITH MAP): Hm?

ME: Which way?! We're coming to a T-junction.

HIM: Er . . . Hang on.

ME: You're reading the map! Or not . . .

HIM: OK, keep your hair on.

ME: Too late!

HIM: Ah. You were supposed to go left there.

ME: How would I know?! SPEAK! You always do this!!

HIM: You should have given me more warning.

ME: You always do this! When I read the map I give you every direction. Twice! Because you can't remember it if I say it forty seconds too early. Then later is too late. And you — when you do it, you fucking drift off!

CHILD IN BACK (CLUTCHING TOY RABBIT): Please don't fight any more.

The last time he did this, sat gazing out of the window with the *A–Z* on his lap, we were going to our friends Rebecca and Tom's. It was all the more infuriating because — being another Efficient Female — Rebecca had actually sent us directions. But Peter failed to read them out in time, so we ended up sailing round the one-way system with apparently no way of getting back. I was so annoyed I threw the directions out of the window and when he got out to retrieve them, drove away.

I know, I know: *awful*. But just think, if we were in the army or something he'd have been put on report — or shot — for putting the rest of the brigade in danger. Did you ever see *Dad's Army*? He was like Private Godfrey. And me, Captain Mainwaring, barking, 'Which way, man? Which way?!' as he gazed dreamily into space. You wouldn't think he'd ever run an entire department, would you? And actually managed people.

As it turned out, the one-way system spat us out only about two streets away, and I did text him which way to go. But when I arrived at Rebecca's with the children I was still fuming, and did that awful thing of coming in muttering irritably, instead of kissing her on both cheeks with a smile. Just to put the icing on it, she was newly engaged at the time. We must have looked like the Before and After of marriage: she and Tom, the gorgeous and charming young couple, and us, the glowering duo, snapping out tight-lipped insults polished by years of practice. Well, I was. Peter managed to make it seem as if it were nothing to do with him. He has this way of coming into a room with his own, self-contained atmosphere, and without apparently saying or doing anything, completely dissociating himself from me. He doesn't look at me in those situations, or answer me. No one ever notices anything; he just keeps smiling and chatting away while I'm silently annihilated by the biological weapon of marriage.

While I was writing this, I heard on the *Today* programme that the UK driving test is to be amended to 'make it more like people's actual experience of driving'. And guess what that means? One of the additions will be that examinees will be asked to follow some brief directions. Can you believe it? According to the Chief Examiner, they'll give them a simple instruction, like: 'Turn left here, then take the first right, followed by the second left.'

And when listeners were still considering the implications of *that*, they may have also been wondering why Evan Davies *didn't* ask:

Is this is a plot by the Ministry of Transport to fail thousands of women, or — and if this is the case, for God's sake, let's give them due credit — is it an Equal Opportunities Commission sponsored initiative to prove that there is no difference in directional sense between women and men? In which case, *good*. Or — and this is a sinister yet strangely attractive thought — is it a thinly veiled attempt to level the playing field — there is a *tiny* difference in the pass rate between 48.6 per cent of male learners and 42.1 per cent of females — by including something, i.e. asking for directions, that men never do?

There was some vague comment from the Examiner about the real issue being what if, say, the learner tries to turn right from the left-hand lane. But you could feel Evan's incredulity, since — and I just *know* this is what he was thinking — men will inevitably fail the new test as they don't ever *ask* for directions, so how can they possibly *follow* them?

This is even without the absurd challenge of trying to test anyone — male or female — on a skill that is so difficult to master. I mean, the whole thing about driving is that it's mechanical. You use your brain and intuition, of course, as in when you just *know* that the person coming towards you in the souped-up Golf with the blacked-out windows and bone-shattering sound system is going to turn right in front of you with no warning. However, most of it develops along neural pathways anchored to certain physical motions that make it, once learned, virtually impossible to forget. It's the reason why if you go back to your old town after years and years, you can still find your way to your school. It's in there, along with the taste of pear drops and the words to the song that was playing when you had your first snog.

But directions? In a test? Let's be honest here. Leaving issues of gender and marriage aside, because so often reaching your destination becomes so much less vital than proving your other half wrong, how many times have you asked the way and actually *taken in what the person said*? Getting directions is what they should test you on in MI5. How to memorize the route from Baghdad to Damascus without being distracted by unrelated hand signals, the contact's nationality, what that sequence of bangs and hisses they're listening to on their iPod means, and your child repeatedly demanding — if they're Lydia — 'I'm not saying I'm going to *buy* that cuddly sloth in the window of that shop we passed twenty minutes ago; I just want to go back and see how *much* it is.'

But in a driving test? Why stop there? Why not 'replicate the experience of real driving' by sending shoals of cyclists to criss-cross in front of you, a schoolboy to wander out with his back to you showing off to his friends — because being run over is so cool, right? — and a really old person with no peripheral vision looking for a parking space. Then all you have to add, to Replicate that Real Experience, is a couple of kids in the back squabbling over a bag of crisps which they spill all over the seat and another adult, say a husband, to explain that there was a really good space back there — which he is now pointing out, fifty yards later — but, being a fundamentally inadequate human being, you missed it.

33

It's Not like Buying a Car
(*Stephen*)

Peter and I met Stephen through the children's school. And over the five years we've known him we've all become close. He is unflinchingly honest and clear-sighted about himself and his motives in life. He's also kind, charming, glib, clever, pedantic, very well informed and the nearest thing I have to a brother: an irritating little brother I quite often want to slap.

Recently he said to me,

'The point of marriage is someone to argue with. I haven't got anyone to argue with so I pick on the children. You must have noticed.'

'Er, no,' I say, since he is one of the most laid-back parents I know.

Well, isn't everyone compared with me? But in six years of friendship I've only seen him lose his temper about twice. And he's incredibly unanxious, which is surprising considering what he's been through. The first time we ever went to the park together, Lucy fell out of a tree and scratched her leg all the

265

way down. He was extremely calm, almost nonchalant, in a way I rather envied. And she, as a result, got over it much sooner. In a world where parents fuss endlessly over their children, and pander to their whims to the point of absurdity, he is a veritable gust of fresh air.

But that's not why I've put him in this book. He is unusual in that he found his Dream Woman, and married her. And before he could discover that she was imperfect, and had smelly feet and annoying habits like anyone else, she died.

So first, let's just find out how a very bright but essentially gentle type like him bagged a woman like Alice, a high-flying lawyer and Alpha Female. After all, he's not one of those men who'll screech up to your side in a Ferrari and leap out with two tickets to Venice. He doesn't show off. If anything, his technique is to disarm you by trying to subvert your expectations — sometimes too much. Instead of openly attempting to impress, he takes pleasure in upsetting your equilibrium. Or maybe he only does this with me.

'Did you always go for alpha females?' I say.

'No, no, not at all. They were very much just girls at school or university or whatever.

My friends were always more important than my relationships.'

Then he met Alice and everything changed. 'She was very dynamic and forthright.'

'And beautiful,' I say. I've seen her picture.

'And well travelled, and articulate, and a top lawyer with a wide network of friends.'

'Whooh.'

'And actually, a very challenging person to go out with,' he adds. 'For her, the relationship was less important than it was for me, who had suddenly found someone I really wanted to spend the rest of my life with.'

'You had met The One.'

'And I wanted her more than she wanted me. I was having to try to impress her, and she was slightly underwhelmed.'

After five years of this, they went up a mountain in Nepal and he whipped out something that stopped her in her tracks.

'I had it all planned: got to the top and got out the ring. And she said yes.'

They got married and had one child, Lucy, then Joe, the second, by which time Alice had begun to show symptoms of what turned out to be an incurable, terminal illness. Stephen nursed her devotedly, but knew he was going to lose her. She died when the children were five and two. He was now a widowed father of two, and he wasn't yet forty.

Five years on, he is in an interesting position compared with other single dads. Unlike most of them, he's not burdened by an antagonistic ex-wife or residual feelings of resentment.

A couple of years ago, a friend of Peter got divorced. The experience was pretty painful and he went around for a while with a dazed look, like someone who had just walked into a door. But one day, he told us he had met someone.

'That was quick!' we said. 'What's she like?'

'Lovely,' he said. 'With lovely kids. It's just her ex-husband that's a problem.'

When they went on dates, it was to court.

Stephen's burdened instead by having already had the ideal woman, to whom no one can be compared. A relationship with anyone else is surely a bit doomed.

'I'm beginning to feel that I'm out on a limb,' he says. 'Most men remarry within five years, don't they? Whereas I can't hold down a relationship.'

He makes himself sound like some feckless Neet[1] lying about smoking dope all day, rather than someone facing an absolutely huge emotional and practical challenge.

---

[1] Not in Education, Employment or Training.

'I used to look at nuclear families and envy them. Now I hear my married friends squabbling about trivia at dinner parties because they haven't got anything more important to worry about.'

Gosh, I do declare he means us.

'So I've gone back to the point of deciding I *can* go it alone. And a relationship would be the icing on the cake, rather than the actual cake.'

'I'd imagine', I say, 'that one of the horrors of dating after a gap of fifteen or so years is that you'd be in such a state about what you look like, and the risk of saying something stupid — you know, being judged.'

In that position now, I'd be terrified of the nightmare of suddenly having to present myself in the best light to a prospective shag, while at the same time thinking: I'm forty-five, why should I try to impress anyone — or care?

'Well, men are much less self-conscious about all that. And I don't find the dates themselves frightening.'

After giving up work to look after the children, he's recently got a job as an IT consultant that he can fit round school hours. I used to love working in offices, partly because it was an opportunity to flirt. Is that still true?

'Well, things are definitely more PC than they were, but in any case, if I go to a meeting or something, they're much younger than me. So that route is sort of closed. And I used to meet women while independently travelling. And of course, with the kids, I don't do that any more.'

He recently answered a lonelyhearts ad. But the effort of organizing the childcare, and being subjected to the curiosity of his family — and Alice's — almost exhausted him before he'd begun.

'Firstly, it took weeks to find a night when she didn't have pilates or Spanish classes or whatever. Then I had to ask one of the family to have the kids for the night, and they wanted to know why. My sister-in-law was curious, because I don't go out much. And then my friends started asking questions . . .'

Whoops, I'm sure we did. I'm quite nosy, obviously, and there's something else I bet he hasn't considered: as my surrogate annoying little brother he's under my protection. If some woman jerks him around, I'll feel it my duty to tell her she doesn't deserve him and to kindly get lost. Well, in my head anyway. But he doesn't evidently feel protected so much as exposed.

'My private life is in the public domain. And my friends can vicariously involve themselves in something they don't do any more, i.e. dating.'

True. We sad married people *love* to hear about other people's romances — fascinating when they go wrong, and when they go well, it's akin to watching something grow, like a lovely pet or plant. I'd count it as one of my hobbies.

'Alice's family have been very good' he says, 'but it's still a huge palaver.'

'Basically it was a whole month of planning and organizing, to get precisely nowhere.'

'But what was she like?'

'The ad said: 'Petite, professional, graduate, well travelled, articulate' . . . '

'Was she a bit of a troll? I gather people lie like hell in these things.'

'No! She was everything she said in the ad, but there was no spark at all.'

Hmm, it does sometimes take time to ignite. I pretty well know that if I don't fancy them *too* much at the start, the relationship has a fighting chance.

'I just knew it wasn't going to work. I'm not sure what the etiquette is these days, but I paid for dinner partly out of guilt that I knew it wasn't going to work. But I did agree to go on a second date . . . '

'Why?!'

'Well, to give it a fair chance, you know. I

didn't want her to feel hurt and rejected.'

'Except that you were going to reject her anyway, just later.'

Men.

'True, I suppose. Ironically, I think one reason we got on quite well is because I didn't feel I had to try.'

There, you see? The best men I ever had were the ones I initially designated as mates. The problem with lusting after someone too much at the outset is that it totally buggers up your judgement. Ask a politician.

Anyhow. There was another issue. Or rather, *the* issue.

'I was probably subconsciously comparing her to Alice,' he admits.

'When you've had the Perfect Person in your life, no one else can match up,' I say.

'Well . . . you can use that to avoid doing it again, to push people away. I've been accused of not wanting to move forward, of still idolizing her.'

'But so what if you do?' I say. 'They may want commitment but why should you offer it? It's not as though you have to prove anything. And they are choosing you, after all, a man with this very particular past.'

'Yes, but in my relationships there's always such a lot of baggage.'

Last year, he had Alice's name tattooed on

his arm, so it might be fair to say the memory isn't exactly fading. And how could it? Why should it? If I were him and someone told me to 'move on', I'd tell them where to go. People who say that are thinking of themselves, not him.

What he's found is that women — even women in a similar situation, for example, divorced with kids — have very different expectations.

'I'd assumed that with someone in the same situation, with the same 'baggage' as it were, there'd be a mutual understanding.'

'Definitely.'

'But the interesting thing I've found is that women don't seem to want a loose, casual arrangement. They feel that if you sleep with them, you have to have 'serious intentions'.'

'You've just discovered this?'

He sees my mouth gawping dramatically open.

'Well, yes.'

'You've just discovered that women generally don't like being involved unless there's an emotional element and it's all leading somewhere, to something permanent?'

'Well, yes.'

'God, man! Where have you been?!'

In a marriage, of course, but not since he was ten. He had been out with people before.

And just to underline the point, I spoke to a divorced friend recently who said she did have a relationship at one point, 'just for the sex', and her other friends disapproved massively:

'When I said I wasn't in love with him, they were appalled.'

What decade are we in? I'm with her. If I was on my own now, with the kids, and like Stephen with my best relationship almost certainly behind me, I'd do the same: have a friendly arrangement of occasional shagging with someone I liked. Who could replace Peter? 'Who'd put up with you?' he always says. But there's another thing.

'I have one or two not entirely lovely memories of men coming into the flat, whom my mother was dating,' I tell him, 'and sort of invading it.'

The thought of anyone dictating to Lawrence and Lydia, or moving their stuff — taking any of their cards off the mantelpiece for instance — makes me feel almost faint. It's surely bound to be a sensitive area, when you've been a tight unit of three for a while.

And of course statistically, men do tend to remarry far sooner after a bereavement, in large part because they're supposedly so dependent. They can't cope on their own, or they *think* they can't; the culture *tells* them they can't. Peter's father could. Stephen can, perfectly well. But if their children suffer, they often stick their heads in the sand. You stop ten newly remarried men in the street and ask them how it's going and how their kids feel about it and eight of them will immediately say, 'Fine!' You think the kids will all say the same? So that would be my other reason for not wanting anything too 'full on'.

Stephen says nothing at all, which I'm hoping means it hasn't been a problem.

He explains why he thought the 'loose, casual arrangement' could be made to work.

'They'd all been married before, knew it wasn't 'till death do us part', yet were so keen to rush into it again.'

'That's women for you,' I say. 'We're idiots.'

'They wanted me to commit in some way before they invested more time in the relationship. They had a specific agenda. And I tried to say to them, maybe it'd be better to take things more slowly and not look at the situation as 'bi-polar' if you like . . . '

Interesting choice of phrase.

'You know, not: *either* it has a future *or* it's all hopeless. It could be somewhere in the middle.'

'I'm with you,' I say. 'Totally.'

'The trouble with it is,' he concludes, 'it's not like buying a car.'

'Well, no.'

'With cars, you get your first one, and the exhaust falls off before you get it out of the garage. But you learn as you go along. Whereas with relationships, you go back to making the same mistakes as when you were a teenager.'

God, no! Anything but that. I'd rather have my head pulled off. Or, indeed, stay married.

34

That Sinking Feeling — Again

'Look, all I want is for you to just acknowledge my point of view. Why won't you? Why?'

Guess where we are. Again.

'You don't give me a chance. You just fly off the handle, spreading your anger all over the place. There's no room for anything else.'

'That is so not true! I explain the situation, or say, 'I'm upset about this,' and you immediately dismiss it.'

'I don't. How can I, when I can't get a word in over your ranting?'

'I don't rant! It's your dismissive attitude that makes me upset in the first place — even more than the thing itself!'

I look across to see if the counsellor is bored. On the contrary, he appears to be mildly amused.

'And part of it is that you dismiss it by saying there's no evidence.'

We're really getting to it now: a pernicious technique of his, which I just *know* is really male, trashing the things that concern me on the grounds that they're not real.

'Say I come in and say, 'Everyone's really pissed off about the junction at the top of the road.' You dismiss it because I don't have a list of individual names and signed statements from each one.'

'No, I don't. But you do make these sweeping claims.'

'But so what? It's just what the neighbours are saying. We're not in court.'

This just elicits a Look. I glance across at the counsellor. I want him to be fair and objective, of course, but also to take my side.

'Or I say that Judy saw those women being mean to that mother who came from the other school; you just wouldn't have it.'

'It's all hearsay.'

'Right. So on that basis the Second World War didn't happen because you weren't bloody there to see it.'

'I'm not even going to answer that.'

I'm sure I detected a smirk from the counsellor then.

'You don't believe anything you haven't personally witnessed, and you especially don't believe it if it comes from me,' I tell him.

'That's just not true. D'you want a list of all the things I've believed that you've told me?'

He shakes his head. We're getting nowhere.

'At least I admit I have anger,' I say. 'You pretend you don't, which is totally dishonest.'

'We all have anger,' says the counsellor. 'You'd agree with that, wouldn't you, Peter?'

'Of course.'

'That's not what you do, though,' I say. 'You pretend you don't. You say things like, '*Sorry*, I don't believe in going down to the bank or wherever and shouting at them' — as if I want you to do that. Which I don't. It's so sarcastic.'

'Well, I'm sorry, I just think that when people lose their temper they're not effective.'

'There you go again. He's doing it again. I'm not asking you to lose your temper!' I say, losing my temper. 'I just want you to acknowledge the validity of what I'm saying.'

'Well, I just remember that when my father lost his temper he lost control and sounded weak.'

'So WHAT?! That's got nothing to do with it. NO ONE IS ASKING YOU TO LOSE YOUR TEMPER!'

'And I'd have thought,' he continues sanctimoniously, 'that having witnessed your father's rages, you'd have been put off that behaviour for life.'

'I DO NOT WANT YOU TO LOSE YOUR TEMPER!'

Now do you see what I mean?

And on the occasions when he does lose it, do you know what he always says?

'Happy now?'

So: wouldn't you want to kill him too?

35

A Day Out

Spring. We're spending the weekend near the seaside, and bored and fidgety, get in the car for a day out. We're going to visit one of those gentrified resorts; another family at school has a cottage there and say it's lovely. But we leave late, at almost noon, and Lawrence already has low blood sugar. He and I have the sort of metabolism where we have to eat six times a day, and Lydia and Peter have the other kind, where they can go for a week on an apple.

Then, just as I realize Lawrence really *has* to eat, like *now*, we hit a traffic jam. The sea is only thirty minutes away, but it's already taken us half an hour and we've only gone a mile up the road.

'Right, we have to find food! It's nearly lunch-time,' I say, resenting the fact that I'm always the one to have to point it out, and annoyed with myself because the only thing in my bag is a chocolate wafer which is completely the wrong thing. But in desperation I push it over the seats. It restores

Lawrence's sugar levels for about four seconds before they plummet again and he is writhing in agony on the back seat. And anyway, I have to give half to Lydia to avoid an even bigger row.

We turn off the main road to avoid the jam.

'This is taking *ages*,' says Lydia.

'Who wanted to go to the seaside anyway?' says Lawrence.

'I did,' I say. 'So we wouldn't be cooped up in the house, getting on each other's nerves.'

'Come on, it'll be lovely!' says Peter. 'We're nearly there.'

'There's a shop,' I say. 'Let's get something there.'

But he drives past. This is a particular failing of his, which has driven me more frequently to the edge of sanity than almost anything else — except his habit of saying, 'Happy now?' whenever I 'make him' lose his temper. But the way he ignores my request, the sheer *infuriatingness* of the way he sails past the shop, makes me want to shove his head through the glass.

'What are you DOING?!'

'It's almost lunchtime. I thought you said we were going for lunch!'

He still *refuses* to understand about Lawrence and food.

'I meant, to get something to keep him

going. He can't last till then! Don't you understand?'

Then I spot a sweet little thatched tea room up ahead. It has a blackboard outside listing just the sort of quick meals we need, and lovely little gingham curtains. All it needs is Snow White to pop round the door with a broom.

'That looks perfect. There — no — what are you *doing*?'

'Going to the seaside,' he says through gritted teeth. 'Isn't that what you wanted?'

'Surely we should have lunch, because everyone is *hungry* — except *you* of course — *then* look at the sea when we've eaten.'

I say this in the passive-aggressive voice that I have learned from him. He has no idea how close I am to killing him right now.

'Right, there's a pub,' he says.

It has a sign outside advertising 'Two Meals for the Price of One', and Karaoke.

'What?' I say. 'What was wrong with that tea room you drove past? You're always saying you don't want them eating junk food. Well, that's exactly what you'll get in there!'

'Right!'

He does a horrendously sharp U-turn and stamps on the gas, and just as I cry,

'There's a speed camera!' I see a flash.

'Happy now?' he says.

Snorting at each other like bulls, we enter the sweet little thatched tea room which, once we get inside, turns out to be a freezing, empty barn.

'My God, it's colder in here than outside,' says Lawrence.

We huddle together in our seats. There are no other customers.

'Could we have some menus?' I ask a woman in a stained T-shirt as she hurries past.

'I'm just coming!' she replies, with an almost audible 'tch'.

'And' — I give her a huge, Joanna Lumley smile — 'could you possibly put the fire on?'

There is a coal-effect gas fire behind a screen, which she grudgingly switches on, carefully keeping the screen in place to make sure none of the heat seeps out.

We open the menus. There is no sign of the cream teas or snack meals listed outside on the jolly-looking blackboard, and everything is absurdly expensive.

'Good choice,' says Peter. 'Thank God we didn't go to the place with two meals for the price of one.'

Whatever he orders, I hope it chokes him.

'Soup,' I say. 'They have soup!'

It's tomato and vegetable. By some miracle, both the children agree to have it

284

and it's quite good. I contemplate ordering another round, but at £4.50 for about a cupful, it's not really on.

'What's for pudding?' says Lawrence.

'We'll have it somewhere else,' we say simultaneously, the only thing we agree on being our desire to get away.

We come out and drive to the sea, staring resolutely ahead as if in the belief that we can leave our dreadful mood behind. But nothing improves, and the water is grey, with nothing else to look at but a grim bit of concrete path facing a deeply uninviting beach. Where's the charming promenade, the bijou little cottages? It's as if we're poisoning our surroundings like a virus as we go.

We don't even bother to get out of the car, but turn round and go on to Chichester, where we warm up with unreasonably expensive hot chocolates — with individually overpriced marshmallows — in a Maison Blanc. Peter and I order without looking at each other, then settle to read bits of the local paper in silence. The two coffees and two hot chocolates with marshmallows in here cost almost as much as the entire lunch at the other place, so to limit the marital fallout further, I grab the bill and pay without letting him see it.

On the way out Lydia says:

'Mummy, if you do get a divorce, bagsy I live with you.'

And on that heart-warming note, we head home.

36

Nice and Here
(*Lawrence*)

Lawrence is now twelve. One Saturday morning we have a chat.

'Will you get married?' I ask him.

'Yes,' he says. 'Hopefully.'

'What will it be like, d'you think?'

'If I make the right choice, good.'

'How do you make the right choice?'

'Don't get married too young.'

'How do you know if it's the right person?'

'Instinct.'

'What are you looking for? What d'you think's important?'

'Agreement on most subjects. Then again, I like debating.'

'On what? What would you talk about with your wife?'

'Politics. Furniture styles. Art.'

Furniture styles?

'Is it easy being married?'

'No. Never easy. Ever.'

This is a little too emphatic. I feel a sting of guilt.

'Why? Is it because we argue so much?'

'Partly.'

Shit.

'Do your friends' parents have better marriages?'

'No.'

That's a relief.

'They all argue sometimes. Jack's parents' marriage is quite peaceful but then his dad is away most of the time. I'd rather have a dad who's here and argues than a dad who's nice but away.'

'Except your dad is nice *and* here!'

'You know what I mean, Mummy.'

'Are you going to have children?'

'Yes.'

He has talked in positive terms about being a father from an early age: when he was about six he told me that one day he would have ten children, all of them called Ben.

'What sort of a father will you be?'

'Considerate — I'll aim to be. Sensitive. Helpful.'

'Say you've got a marvellous job. Will you give it up to look after them?'

'It depends. If it's a job I like and it pays well, I'll try to keep it.'

It's as if he's really thought about this, and — which seems extraordinary to me — has a clear vision of himself as an adult.

288

When I was twelve I had no ambition beyond staying up past nine o'clock and getting to wear heels.

'Can you imagine being the one who stays at home?' I say.

'Yes. I know how to cook.'

I raise a sceptical eyebrow.

'I will, I mean. And at some point I'll probably babysit someone so I should know what to do by then.'

I gaze at him, wondering how, amid all the anxiety and strife, we've managed to produce such a mature, rounded child. Lydia's not bad either.

'You're a lovely boy,' I say, kissing him. 'Promise me one thing?'

He sighs warily.

'What?'

'If you do marry, promise me you'll choose someone who loves you as much as I do.'

'God,' he says. 'Do I have to hear this again? Can't I just have a hug without getting any Tips on Life?'

'Oh. Have I said it before?'

'Only, like, fifty times.'

'Sorry.'

'Yeah, whatever. Can I go now?'

I take my tea into the other room and sit beside Peter.

'Your son is amazing,' I tell him.

'I know. I just can't imagine life without them, though.'

But imagine it we must.

37

Risk Assessment

It's May. Half-term is almost upon us and Lydia is going to join Lawrence on his school canoeing trip. I must go round the neighbourhood gathering wet-suits. Not counting weekends with Peter's sister and her husband, they've never both been away without either of us.

They're going to paddle, cook and camp out, and Peter and I are going to a B&B on the South Downs. His job is to help them pack, while I run through a random list of disasters that have befallen children on school trips.

'And what about that girl who drowned off the coast of Dorset? She was in a canoe.'

'Yeah. They'll be fine.'

'And then there were those kids who were swept away in some river not that long ago. They weren't even — '

'Yeah. They'll be fine.'

And he says *I* interrupt all the time.

Because they've never been away together like this, I cannot yet see beyond the wall of generalized anxiety that surrounds my being, so the childless future is as yet unglimpsed. I can only imagine four of us, not two.

We take them to school, wave them off in their minibus and drive down to Sussex.

'We're off the leash,' says Peter. 'We can do anything!'

So we go crazy, with coffee and the papers, then a two-hour lunch, followed by a slow dawdle round the bookshops of Lewes, topped off by a fabulous dinner with drinks on a terrace. The thrill is almost too much.

'You do realize,' says Peter, 'that this is the future.'

And, stupid as it sounds, it slowly dawns on me, with the shattering enormity of a tidal wave, that I've never thought about it before.

The children are going to grow up.

They are going to become *adults*.

And they are going to *move out*. Probably. Eventually. If they — and we — can afford it.

And he and I are going to be alone together, probably for quite a long time. I mean, I hope for a long time.

And we will no longer have that distraction — all these distractions; we will just have each other.

Why did I not see this before?

Before Lawrence learned to speak, obviously we knew he would; we just couldn't imagine it. Before he learned to read, we knew he would, but we couldn't quite imagine that either. The same went for doing up his own shoes, pouring his own drinks and answering back.

With Lydia it was easier because we'd seen Lawrence do all these things first. Yet even despite that I look at them both now, and cannot envisage them living independently of us. And therefore, I cannot imagine us living without them. We did it before, I know. But we were fresher then. We hadn't heard all each other's stories. We hadn't rolled our eyes and said, 'I know' before the other had got halfway through a sentence.

I feel really panicky. And I start doing what I always do when I feel panicky: I immediately call to mind something that will make me feel a lot worse. I remember the couple in a documentary whose five-year-old wouldn't stay in bed. He came downstairs and interrupted whatever his parents were doing, every single night. And once they'd gone to bed, he appeared in their room and got in with them, every single night. And in the programme they were given a parenting manual to follow, and encouraged to carry him back to his own bed. No matter how many times he came in — and it was up to thirty-five times *a night* — they had to pick him up and take him back. And they did it. By the end of four weeks he was sleeping through the night in his own bed. And his parents had got their evenings back. And they split up.

So I'm quite apprehensive.

In fact, part of me is terrified.

On the other hand, all this eating and browsing is *really nice.* We go at the same pace, and if one of us wants to spend longer in a particular shop, leafing through old transport manuals, say, the other does not sigh or nag because they may be in another shop admiring cookware, or dresses that look fine on the hanger but will invariably not fit.

So there is a paradox. I'm scared of the children leaving home because I'll miss them, and I know Peter feels the same. And I'm worried about the years ahead in case we spend them arguing, and he has expressed a fear of that too. But I also notice with a jolt how well we're getting on. Virtually the moment the minibus pulled out of the school gates, our mood improved. And that seems awful.

'We're getting on so much better, aren't we, now that they're away. Do you feel guilty too?' I say.

'I know what you mean, but no,' says Peter. 'Look: homemade biscuits!'

Normally my brain would cut out at the word biscuits. But I'm thinking about how, when I asked for a large room, it turned out to be the family room, which as well as the generous double, has an extra single and a sofa-bed. It seems to illustrate our situation.

'It's as if they were here, and now they're gone.'

'But they'll come back.'

I know he's right. And besides, I have enough to worry about. In the meantime, I guess we'll just have to start with these two days, then take it one step at a time.